TEACHING AND ASSESSING
IN NURSING PRACTICE

or before

TEACHING AND ASSESSING IN NURSING PRACTICE

An Experiential Approach

NEIL KENWORTHY BEd RGN RMN RNT

Director of Nurse Education
North Lincolnshire School of Nursing

PETER J NICKLIN MEd DipEd(Lond) RGN RMN RNT

Director of Nurse Education
York and Scarborough School of Nursing

Foreword by
EVE BENDALL MA PhD SRN RNT

Lately Chief Executive Officer
English National Board
London

SCUTARI PRESS
London

First published 1988
Reprinted 1989, 1990, 1991

ISBN 1 871364 15 9

Typeset by Inforum Ltd, Portsmouth
Printed and bound in Great Britain by
Biddles Ltd, Guildford and King's Lynn

Contents

Foreword

Nurses, for decades, have been ambivalent concerning the role of supervisor, teacher and assessor of students in the clinical situation. Forty years ago, no-one doubted that trained nursing staff on wards and departments were the most suitable people to undertake this role. Thirty years ago, with the beginning of growth in the numbers of nurse teachers, this view began to be challenged. Twenty years ago, it was realized that nurse teachers could not fulfil the demands of the situation and the grade of clinical teacher was introduced. During the last ten years it has become clear that, in many places, clinical teachers are being used to work with students currently in the School of Nursing rather than with those working in the clinical areas, and that the latter (much larger) group are still unsupported except by their student colleagues. Subsequently, two decisions have been taken. The first, to introduce short courses on 'teaching and assessing in clinical practice' for trained staff working in clinical areas when students are training; this is a formal acknowledgement of the fact that since the teacher does not practice, the practitioner must be enabled to teach. The second decision has been to phase out courses preparing nurses to be 'full-time' clinical teachers. The wheel has come full circle.

This book aims to provide 'a resource for all those involved with the education and training of nurses in the practical setting'. Its production is timely, and its content will meet the needs of three groups: firstly, all those who have undertaken ENB Course 998, or an equivalent, who, when the course is over, find it vital to refer to a definitive text when faced with the real situation; secondly, those actually undertaking the course — and those organising such courses; and thirdly, those who have as yet not had the opportunity to take such a course. The book covers, thoroughly and explicitly, the areas in which trained staff experience problems when trying to meet the needs of student nurses.

The authors are leading nurse educators who each have the added advantage that they have actually experienced the 'partnership' between a school of nursing and an institution of higher education in one of the 'pilot schemes' approved by the English National Board for Nursing, Midwifery and Health Visiting; participation in the scheme has also enabled them to begin to understand, at first hand, what it means when a student nurse — if only for a short time — is a student and not a worker. The second of these two changes will, to some degree, become a reality for all during the next decade. The first – the 'partnership' — *must* develop further if nurse training is to become nurse education in anything but name.

Neil Kenworthy and Peter Nicklin belong to the generation of Directors of Nurse Education in whose hands will lie the greatest transition ever envisaged for nurse training. It is encouraging that their first book shows a deep understanding of the needs of students in the place where nursing actually 'happens'. Many will benefit from this book and it is to be hoped that other publications will follow.

EVE BENDALL
1988

Preface

Amongst the large number of advances in nursing education during the past decade two stand out as being particularly significant: firstly, the rapid growth in the field of postbasic education, accompanied by the provision of increased resources and, secondly, the much heightened awareness of the need for the qualified nurse to receive adequate preparation for the teaching and assessing of students.

Many postbasic courses for registered nurses contain a teaching objectives element, particularly those concerned with 'developments in nursing'. Qualified nurses have received preparation for teaching and assessing in a number of ways: either informally through in-service training activities which may have included 'art of examining' courses or, more formally, through the very popular City and Guilds Further Education Teacher's Certificate course. Many nurses have received no preparation at all.

In writing this book the authors have sought to produce a resource for all those involved with the education and training of nurses in the practical setting; as a framework for the book the outline curriculum of the English National Board's Course 998 — Teaching and Assessing in Clinical Practice — has been used. A dilemma faced when designing the content of the book concerned the balance between theory and practice. Whilst not wanting to produce a 'workshop manual' on how to teach and assess, the authors were equally anxious not to end up with a book top heavy with theory and of very little practical value. Using the principle that 'there is nothing as practical as sound theory' the authors have endeavoured to provide a resource that will be of value to the 'knowledgeable doer' in preparation for the mentorship role. Their judgement is based upon personal experiences as teachers on both Further Education Teacher's Certificate (City and Guilds 730) and Certificate in Education courses, in addition to perceiving the needs of qualified nurses who are supervising students in the English National Board's pilot schemes in general nurse training. By adapting the experiential approach to teaching and learning described by Steinaker and Bell to nursing education and training, the authors believe that integration of theory with practice has a better chance of occurring — an educational principle which is so necessary in the practical setting. Not all nurses have a responsibility for the supervision of students, but there is an ever-increasing recognition of the nurse as an advocate, health adviser and health educator to patients, clients and relatives. The same obviously applies to those nurses who do carry out a teaching and assessing role with students. Perhaps this book therefore has a dual utility; primarily to serve as a resource and guide to the qualified nurse in the mentorship role with students and, secondarily, to assist the nurse in fulfilling the broader role of health educator to all.

NEIL KENWORTHY
PETER J NICKLIN
1988

Note: The term 'nurse' is used to simplify the presentation but midwife or health visitor can be substituted in all cases. Similarly, where 'student' is used, the term 'pupil' is equally applicable.'

1
Introducing the Experiential Approach

The vocational nature of nurse education has always required that trained nurses should act as supervisors and instructors for those in training. Whether those undertaking a training in nursing are part of the N H S workforce or 'students' supernumerary to the manpower equation they will continue to require the mentorship of competent role models. It is self-evident that a basic nurse education does not adequately equip nurses for their teaching and assessing role, particularly at a time when nursing and nurse education is subject to radical reform. Without dedicated training, qualified nurses are unable fully to exercise this role and students are potentially denied appropriate teaching and learning opportunities. This inevitably has implications for the quality of nurse training and, ultimately, for the quality of care delivered to patients and clients.

It is with cognisance of the need to improve standards of teaching and assessing in clinical practice that the English National Board for Nursing, Midwifery and Health Visiting has published *Outline Curricula* to help staff involved in teaching and supervising students. This book is intended to augment such courses; however, it is hoped that its style, content and presentation will provide practical assistance to all those who have a responsibility for teaching and assessing of nursing. The major themes of discussion are:

— The principles and practice of teaching, learning and assessing in clinical practice
— Factors that create a supportive learning environment
— An introduction to basic counselling skills in the context of nurse education
— Recording and reporting on students' progress and development and
— Contemporary developments in nursing education

In attempting to discuss these and related issues, the authors are aware that depth is being sacrificed for breadth of coverage. However, this book is not intended as a definitive source of reference but as an introductory companion and guide. They advocate an experiential approach to teaching and assessing.

The term 'experiential' is used increasingly to describe a variety of approaches. What happens in some activities labelled 'experiential' is sufficiently different in character, purpose and outcome from others similarly described that it is hardly surprising if the term itself arouses confusion, anxiety and even hostility. In this respect Taylor (1983) has a word of caution: 'Experiential Learning is in danger of becoming yet one more educational fashion attracting a good deal of momentary attention, achieving a brief period of fashionable acceptance and little lasting acceptance.' 'Experiential' when used here in this text refers to the application of the 'experiential taxonomy' as developed and described by Steinaker & Bell (1979). The authors' motivation for exploring this approach is their awareness that, whilst nurse education is developing courses that are consistent with contemporary health care demands and the nursing role, there has been a potential to ignore contemporary advances in curriculum design.

Over thirty-five years ago educationists, in an attempt to identify and measure learning outcomes, devised classifications of learning objectives. These classifications of taxonomies (a taxonomy is a system of hierarchical classification) delineated the consequence of the educative process into three divisions or domains:

1   The *cognitive domain* — the use of information and knowledge
2   The *affective domain* — attitudes, emotions and values
3   The *psychomotor domain* — muscular and motor skills

Readers will be familiar with ward learning objectives being categorised into *knowledge, skills* and *attitudes*. However, the problem with such a classification is that whilst it is self-evident that thinking, feeling and doing are integrated there is a tendency to deal with them in isolation. Nursing education, although very much skills-based, ought not to adopt learning and teaching principles where knowledge, attitude and practical skills are seen as separate learning activities. This danger can be very much reduced or even negated by using an approach to teaching and learning that provides a framework for understanding, planning and evaluating the meaning of total experiences. The authors of this experiential taxonomy not only describe the levels or sequence of events which take the student from inability through to achievement (Table 1.1) but also offer appropriate learning objectives, learning principles, learning strategies, teaching strategies and assessment techniques.

These levels of the experiential approach will be further explored and expanded in the chapters on learning, teaching and assessing but it is necessary at this early stage to say what the experiential taxonomy is not as well as what it is.

The two terms 'experiential taxonomy' and 'experiential learning' are not necessarily synonymous. A curriculum can employ experiential learning without being based on an experiential taxonomy. Similarly, a course built on the experiential taxonomy can use methods other than, or in addition to, experiential approaches. Many teachers' and nurses' perception of experiential learning is confined to role-play, gaming and simulation. An even narrower interpretation of experiential learning is that its sole usage is in relation to 'self-awareness' training. The experiential taxonomy, whilst using experiential learning methods,

Table 1.1   Levels of the experiential taxonomy (after Steinaker & Bell 1979)

1	Exposure level	The student is introduced to and is conscious of an experience
2	Participation level	The student has to make a decision to become a part of the experience
3	Identification level	The student identifies with the experience both intellectually and emotionally
4	Internalisation level	The student progresses to this level when the experience begins to affect her or his life, changing behaviours and ways of doing things
5	Dissemination level	The student now expresses the experience, advocating it to others

is much more than a learning/teaching strategy. It is the taxonomy that is experiential rather than the learning method. This is more than just a subtle or semantic difference, the underlying assumption being that for learning to take place an experience has to be undergone. If this is accepted, the taxonomy is then seen as a series of stages taking the student from initial exposure to the experience through to its ultimate incorporation into the student's observable behaviour. The experience may be a simulated one involving role-play or it may be real, or it may be neither. A formal lecture is an experience, and so is reading a book; both are methods of exposing students to an idea, a piece of information or a concept. Proponents of experiential learning techniques, however, would not recognise these latter examples as having a place in their learning methods.

A curriculum planned on the experiential taxonomy thus uses a whole range of internally compatible teaching and learning strategies. Many of them reflect an experiential learning approach, others are expository or teacher-centred. 'Internal compatibility' is possibly the most significant characteristic of the taxonomy. The authors' experience suggests that there are frequently incompatibilities in course design. For example, assessment methods that aim to measure nursing competencies are frequently measuring a narrow band of cognitive skill, or a particular teaching strategy is used not because it is compatible with the student's current learning style but merely because it is fashionable.

Although the main purpose of this book is to examine some of the principles and practicalities of learning, teaching, assessing and evaluating, it is necessary also to explore some of the associated factors that have an influence upon or are a consequence of these key educational activities. Changes in health care are ever increasing in both quantity and quality. Developments in nursing research and a greater awareness of research amongst nurses are significant features of contemporary health care provision. Similarly, rapid expansion in the fields of postbasic and continuing education for nurses and other health professionals is contributing to change and progress in care delivery. Resources will always be scarce in the health service but those allocated to education at all levels and to the provision of research must be welcomed as a sound investment.

References

Steinaker N & Bell R (1979) *The Experiential Taxonomy: A New Approach to Teaching and Learning.* New York: Academic Press

Taylor B (1983) *Experiential Learning.* N I C E C Hatfield Polytechnic.

2
The Principles of Learning

Introduction

Most nurses, health visitors and midwives can remember their first few days and weeks as raw entrants to training. Whether they commenced their basic courses in a small provincial hospital or in a large nationally known teaching hospital, the message put across by their course tutors was no doubt the same. All students were informed that although they may associate the School of Nursing and its classrooms with learning this was almost insignificant when compared with the amount of learning that would take place outside the classroom and at the bedside with the patient. Indeed, it was instilled into the student that the School of Nursing is much more than those buildings that provide the classroom accommodation — it is the entire hospital and its population.

No doubt nurse teachers today are saying similar things to their student nurses. What was true then still applies now and it is the learning that takes place outside the classroom and within the patient environment that forms the subject for consideration in this chapter.

Rather than dwell upon dictionary meanings of the term 'learning' or the many definitions offered by writers on the subject of education, the description offered by Curzon (1985) is perhaps a useful bench-mark, particularly where learning is taking place in a practical setting. Curzon considers learning as the 'apparent modification of a person's behaviour through his activities and experiences so that his knowledge, skills and attitudes, including modes of adjustment towards his environment, are changed, more or less permanently'. What does this mean when applied to student nurses and their anticipated or required learning in a practical experience placement? It usually means the acquisition of the stated objectives commonly expressed in the form of the cognitive, affective and psychomotor taxonomies, i.e. Bloom (1964), Krathwohl et al (1968) and Simpson (1966). The separation of knowledge, attitudes and physical skills is convenient when designing learning objectives, but is it realistic? Do students learn chunks of knowledge in isolation from having a feeling towards the subject and are physical skills acquired in the absence of any knowledge? Whilst advocating Curzon's definition of learning as a practical proposition for nurse

5

education, it can probably be modified somewhat to remove the artificiality of the three domains, i.e. knowledge, skills, attitudes. The description of learning as applied to nurse education in the practical setting would now read ' . . . the measurable effect of the sum total of the planned and unplanned experiences upon the student, in both quantitative and qualitative terms'. How these responses to experience are measured will form the subject of a separate chapter. It may be appropriate at this stage to refer briefly to some of the more important theories of learning so that practical teachers can make the best use of the learning opportunities as they arise or are engineered within their care environment.

Learning theories

Behaviourism

Under this heading learning is concerned with individuals' response or 'behaviour' to a given stimulus. At the reflex level the reaction is an automatic response to the sensory stimulus and at a slightly higher level the same response can be evoked through the association of a secondary or conditioned stimulus with the unconditioned stimulus. All nurses will recall Pavlov's experiments with salivating dogs. The type of learning is fundamental to habit formation where some signal or stimulus sets off a series of activities, each reaction acting as a stimulus and creating yet another reaction. It may be fashionable to claim that such learning has no place in contemporary nursing education. Should not today's student nurses learn through enquiry, problem-solving, conceptualising theoretical situations and working out practical applications? Yes, of course they should, but is there not also a need for that 'immediate motor response to a sensory stimulus'? Picture the nurse in a sudden, totally unexpected life-threatening situation. Her patient suddenly collapses and there are no vital signs; what nursing behaviours are now required? Does the nurse conceptualise the situation; is there time to consider and analyse the problem? Of course these questions are rhetorical and almost insulting to the reader, but surely they serve to remind teachers that undoubtedly the stimulus–response approach to learning has its place.

Neobehaviourism

Behaviour modification, operant conditioning and positive reinforcement are all terms associated with this approach to learning, the main proponents of which include Skinner and Gagne. Learning, according to Gagne (1983), consists of sequential stages or a hierarchy of phases founded upon prerequisite abilities or intellectual skills. Many of these principles are appropriate to nursing education at the practical level. Ward learning objectives and ward teaching programmes based upon the student's stage in training and level of attainment in previous practical placements are relevant factors compatible with Gagne's view of learning. Additionally, Gagne very much stressed the importance of providing the student with immediate knowledge of performance. Constant communication with the student, planning of feedback and regular evaluation of learning are therefore characteristic features of neobehaviourism. The ward sister or practical supervisor is effecting these principles of learning by carrying out preexperience discussions with the student, identifying strengths and weaknesses, anxieties and expectations. Similar discussions or reviews may take place at specified intervals during the student's placement, and certainly at the end of the experience, where not only is an assessment of progress and attainment completed but also an evaluation of the experience provided for the student.

Gestalt theory of learning

Although very much an oversimplification of what is a complex process the Gestalt approach may be summed up by the phrase 'learning through insight'. More accurately, 'insight' is a fundamental component of the Gestalt learning process rather than a synonym for it — the outcome of the student organising clues or components of a problem so that patterns emerge and solutions occur. This approach to education is very much concerned with problem-solving and discovery-learning methods. To the advocate of Gestaltism the process by which a problem is solved and the learning that takes place during that process is often considered to be as important as the solution or outcome. It sometimes comes as a surprise to the inexperienced student nurse that the signs and symptoms of a particular disease or condition as described in a textbook are very rarely presented in such a way by the real-life patient. The student quickly learns, however, to observe, analyse and put together the clues that form the parts of the whole. With practice, and Gestaltists recognise that practice is important, the student begins to recognise patterns, appreciate relationships and perceive how problems can be solved and new conclusions reached. Thus, learning is based upon awareness and understanding rather than on repetitive or habitual actions. Just as the signs and symptoms of an illness are different in real life in comparison with the textbook description so, too, is the nature and course of the illness when witnessed in different patients. The student should now be able to discriminate between the behaviours of individuals and recognise the key features of an illness even though these may be masked and distorted by the patient's attempts to compensate or counteract the effects of illness.

Cognitive theory of learning

This theory of learning is an extension of the Gestalt approach and seeks to build upon the insights of the student by stimulating the development of perception, understanding of principles and attainment of competences. The term 'cognition' relates to knowledge or knowing as opposed to feelings or activities, although it might be argued that in reality it is difficult if not impossible to isolate these three aspects or domains of behaviour. Compared with the stimulus–response of behaviourist learning, the student of cognitive theory will be attempting to interpret and develop some perception of the stimulus. This may necessitate referral to previous experiences, particularly those that might have had similar stimuli to the current learning situation. Bruner (1964), in supporting this approach, describes the spiral curriculum which, although moving on-wards, also circles back to previous experiences and understandings, building upon them and enhancing the appropriate issues, principles and values. Nurses may recognise the significance of the concept of the spiral curriculum in relation to the nine competences described by Rule 18(1) of the Nurses, Midwives and Health Visitors Rules Approval Order 1983. All basic nursing courses must be designed to fulfil the appropriate learning objectives, learning opportunities and learning activities which will enable the student nurse to achieve and practise the aforesaid competences.

This introduction to learning theories has sought merely to classify the different concepts and provide a framework within which the detailed factors relating to learning can be presented and discussed. Educational courses in nursing, midwifery and health visiting may arguably be described as vocational, in that the student is additionally in most cases an employee contributing to the provision of a health care service. This chapter opened by stating that most learning would take place in the practical setting away from theoretical confines of the classroom. The experience that the student nurse is undergoing might be claimed to be the foundation for this substantial area of learning.

Learning in the practical setting

Nursing education has a long history of providing practical experience for its students which has not always been directly related to the theoretical instruction. In recent years the statutory bodies have required the presence of concurrent theory and practice as a fundamental prerequisite to course approval. Basic nurse training schemes are increasingly becoming skills-based, with associated supportive theory. This has required educational planners to examine alternative models for curriculum building. When courses were heavily knowledge-based and theory preceded practical experience, a curriculum based upon a taxonomy as described by Bloom (1964) was then ideal. The student followed a given theoretical concept through a series of levels, commencing with a basic know-ledge and then progressing through increasingly complex intellectual stages until the highest level of understanding was reached – all this in the absence of any realistic meaningful experience.

An experience-based course does not deny intellectual skills: indeed, the reverse is the case, for it seeks to integrate them with both attitudinal and psychomotor skills to produce a student who can recognise the relationship between thinking, feeling and doing. When a student learns from a particular experience on a hospital ward or in a health care department she does not just learn a piece of knowledge or a physical skill or undergo a feeling in isolation each from the other. Any experience in which the student participates has a degree of knowing, feeling and doing. These three areas of behaviour are commonly referred to as domains — hence, cognitive domain for knowing and understanding, affective domain for feelings and attitudes and psychomotor domain for physical actions or doing.

To try to devise a nursing course using these separate domains of behaviour so that for each subject of the syllabus the knowledge part of it is taught first, then the practical aspects and, finally, the attitudes or feelings about it, may risk being seen as artificial and totally inappropriate for a course that has a strong vocational nature. Steinaker and Bell (1979) describe an approach to teaching and learning that claims not to break down human behaviour artificially into knowing, feeling and doing but to see human experience as a whole, bigger than the sum total of its parts. This closely resembles the gestalt approach to learning and is compatible with Marson's (1979) plea to nurse educators and curriculum planners, reminding them that human behaviour is a holistic process and that all three domains of behaviour need to be integrated in a compatible and complementary manner for relevant learning to occur. Where the main approach to learning consists of deliberate exposure of the student to situations or experiences it is becoming increasingly referred to as 'experiential learning'. If an entire curriculum is based upon a sequence or series of levels of experience for which there are appropriate learning objectives, learning principles and learning strategies, then it is understandable that Steinaker and Bell have called their approach to teaching and learning an 'experiential taxonomy'. There are five such levels of experience in the sequence, commencing with exposure to the situation. Following exposure, which has to be seen as the fundamental basis to learning, there are four other levels, namely participation, identification, internalisation and dissemination. These are now briefly examined.

Exposure to an experience

This first level of learning occurs when the student meets or is introduced to a specific situation. In the health care situation this may involve contact with a patient, visitors, other staff members or a piece of equipment or machinery. At the exposure stage the student is using the senses to gain an appreciation and perception of the experience. Two options face the student; either to reject the experience, which will be difficult if it is a planned part of learning, or to accept further exposure and subsequent interaction. A positive response by the student leads to readiness for participation.

Participation in an experience

This requires the student to become involved physically, emotionally and intellectually. A common practice in nurse education is for the student to rehearse the participation in an artificial or imitation setting prior to carrying out the activity with a patient. This is thought to help in building the confidence of the student, although some teachers may suggest that it is only delaying the inevitable active involvement through which real learning takes place.

Identification with the experience

Successful participation tends to produce emotional satisfaction and with it the desire to repeat the experience. This emotional satisfaction soon gives way to intellectual commitment and the student readily expresses opinions about the experience and is willing to share it with others, i.e. talking about it to colleagues.

Internalisation of the experience

When a new experience is accepted and practised at an intellectual level it begins to be part of the life style of the student, influencing both actions and attitudes. This may be something as simple as wearing a nurse's uniform. The effects may be only transitory to begin with but as reinforcemet occurs the experience becomes intrinsic to the behaviour of the student.

Dissemination of the experience

The desire of the student to talk about and share her new piece of learning with others is already evident. At this final level of learning the student is now seeking to stimulate and inform others to become involved in the experience — she is beginning to teach.

Some associated learning principles

So far, reference has been made in this chapter to the main theories of learning, and the levels or stages through which a student may progress in a practical learning situation have been briefly described. If learning is to be more than an accidental outcome or the result of good intention, then opportunities for learning have to be planned, engineered and resourced. These will be addressed in more detail when the principles of teaching are considered, but if learning is to be meaningful and effective then a number of factors have to be present at the time of the learning experience. Some of these factors are internal or intrinsic to the student, e.g. feelings that are present, whilst other factors are external or extrinsic of the student, e.g. the influence of the environment. Rather than describe these factors or associated learning principles at random, a better appreciation may be achieved if they are examined as they occur at the different levels of the learning experience. For example, exposure to an experience was described as the first level of the learning process. What associated learning principles may be considered as important features at this early stage of the learning process? Certainly, motivation is a key factor and this incorporates such things as the individual's needs and drives, the desire to achieve, fear of failure and how others perceive you.

Motivation, focusing, level of anxiety

Much has been written on the topic of motivation, and the needs satisfaction theory described by Maslow (1970) is probably one with which most nurses will be familiar (Fig. 2.1). This theory suggests that as lower-level needs are fulfilled there will be a drive to satisfy higher-level needs (Fig. 2.2). At the exposure stage of experiential learning, motivation is almost entirely of the extrinsic form and is concerned with creating a drive or a desire within the student to want to learn.

Fig. 2.1   Maslow's hierarchy of human needs (Maslow 1970)

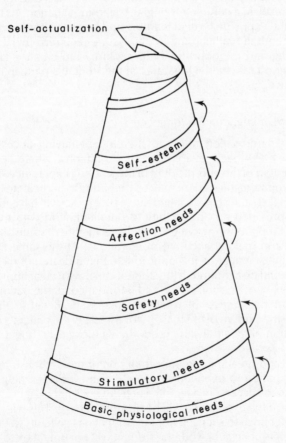

Fig. 2.2   The life spiral of human needs (after Maslow)

For a student nurse, this extrinsic motivation may be provided by enabling observation of a nursing skill being carried out in the practical setting rather than having it described in theory in a classroom.

Focusing is just an extension of motivation — it gives meaning to the stimuli that act as motivators. Using the above example of motivation the nursing supervisor would direct the student's attention to the significant points to note whilst observing the nursing skill being carried out.

Level of anxiety refers to the student's state of emotional arousal. Most new situations have the potential for generating anxiety. This is the body's normal response and is manifest through increased respiration circulation and muscle tone. Such a degree of anxiety is a positive feature of learning, conducive to quick thinking and mental response. An excess amount of anxiety is, of course, detrimental to learning. If the student nurse in our example of observing a particular nursing skill has been told that she will be required to describe her observations to the rest of the student group the anxiety then produced may be so great as to distract her observation and thinking. This will add further to her anxiety and may result in a completely negative learning situation. As the student progresses from the exposure level of learning and begins to participate actively in an experience, additional learning principles are required. Initial guidance, providing meaning and the opportunity to explore, and creating chances for success are all important enabling features of the student's participation in the learning experience.

Initial guidance, meaning, chance for success

Guidance during participation refers to the student having access to good briefing, supportive feedback, examples and illustrations, where appropriate, and a clear perception of the end-product of the learning experience. Within the patient-care environment the student may be preparing to participate in a patient assessment for the first time. The qualified nurse supervisor will have fully briefed the student and provided an opportunity for familiarisation with the relevant documentation. Preparatory activities may have included some rehearsal at asking questions and making accurate observations. At the same time as the student receives initial guidance it is appropriate that a degree of meaning and understanding should be acquired. If the student can have a clear appreciation of the learning experience, its significance and importance, participation will then be enhanced and the degree of retention increased. Because there is an understanding by the student of the reasons for assessing the patient's needs and how the information obtained will be used, the whole activity ought then to be that much more effective.

Both guidance and meaning are important contributors to ensuring that the student has the chance to experience success in the new learning situation. Where the chance to succeed in a learning activity does not exist or is very slim, then participation in the experience will be non-productive. This will also be the case if there is the chance to succeed but the student has difficulty in recognising it. When success has been achieved, the student will not only seek to repeat the activity which brought about the success but will aspire to further learning experiences of a similar nature. In the practical learning environment this may consist of the student repeating the activity with a different subject, i.e. carrying out an assessment on a different patient, or reassessing the same patient at a subsequent date, but this time with less guidance or supervision.

The emotional warmth and feeling of self-satisfaction that accompany success are very significant factors in the movement of the student from the level of participation in a learning experience to the level at which identification with the experience begins to take place. It is through having specific feelings about an experience in the first place that the student can begin to examine it at an intellectual level. The learning principles which Steinaker associates with student identification with a learning experience are the personal interaction of that student, the knowledge of results and constant reinforcement.

Personal interaction, knowledge of results, reinforcement

The successful participation in a new experience has involved the development of an understanding and has created positive feelings. Examination of that experience at an intellectual level has been made possible. Personal involvement with an experience is characterised by the desire to discuss it with others and further increase understanding. Having successfully carried out the patient care assessment, the student will wish to talk about the experience to other nurses. A rapport will have been created between the student and the patient and the desire to spend more time with the patient will be evident. This results from the student's feeling of now being personally involved with the patient and the need to acquire a deeper understanding about him.

Knowledge of results provides the student with insights into achievement, or lack of it, whichever the case may be. When the student can see the completed patient care assessment being used by the members of the nursing team as a basis for care planning, this represents a positive outcome. The student has evidence that learning has been successful and is acknowledged as such not only by peers but by superiors.

Reinforcement is essential at this level of learning to ensure that practices resulting in positive and successful outcomes become a permanent feature of the student's professional behaviour. Skills transference is beginning to take place at this stage and a good reinforcement strategy for the student nurse who is learning to assess patients' needs is to ensure that 'practice' is gained with patients who have different dependencies and needs. This will help to develop the newly acquired skills and create further opportunity for success. Reinforcement as a learning principle facilitates the transition from the level of identification with the experience to that of its internalisation. Repeated practice in a wide variety of settings has ensured that what was an intellectual commitment to the activity is now becoming an automatic part of nursing behaviour.

Overlearning, transfer (intrinsic), differentiation

The internalisation of a learning experience occurs with the incorporation of the experience into the student's life style, with the potential to influence feelings, attitudes and beliefs. This may be witnessed in its more overt presentation in, for example, the area of health education. The student nurse, having been exposed to the concept of the nurse as a health educator, has begun to participate actively in behaviours such as healthy eating, regular exercise, stopping smoking and mental relaxation. Having found this new life style beneficial, the student becomes committed to its principles and advocates them to others. As a role model for healthy living the student is providing evidence of the internalisation of specific learning experiences. What then is meant by overlearning? It sounds a somewhat derogatory term but, in fact, it is a very important principle of most learning processes. Overlearning is a type of reinforcement that gives the student the confidence and authority that comes with knowing or doing something very well. With overlearning the student is completely familiar with the skill or piece of knowledge and can use it readily. Now part of the work behaviour, it will be retained for future use and, in addition, become the foundation for transference to other activities. The student who has developed the skill of assessing patients' needs will be able to use the principles of assessment for problem solving in a wide range of different circumstances. Transfer of learning may best be described as a higher activity of the internalisation process and typified by the student's ability to build upon established knowledge and skills for the development of new skills, and to formulate further concepts. This broadens the student's repertoire of experience and enables the conscious awareness of utilising or testing acquired knowledge in new situations. Having analysed the ability to assess patients' needs and plan appropriate care, the student may wish to see if the same skills are applicable to other aspects of life. Will the professional skills apply in personal and social life? All basic nursing courses require the student to follow a planned sequence of different practical placements designed to provide a well-balanced appreciation of the caring specialisms and varied client groups. This programme of experiences also facilitates the learning principle of differentiation. After a period of two or three months of caring for adult patients undergoing surgical treatment, the student may be placed in a day care centre which provides a facility for people with mental health problems. Can the student make adjustments to recently acquired knowledge and skills to meet the demands of this new learning environment? If the ability to analyse, assess and plan has been successfully internalised the student will quickly adapt to the new situation.

Returning to the student nurse who has adjusted her life style to reflect the total concept of healthy living, at the highest level of learning not only does the experience influence the behaviour of the individual but she actively seeks to convince others of its merits and worth. This level of learning is referred to as *dissemination*, and its associated learning principles are *transfer* (extrinsic), *reward* and *motivation* (internal).

At this highest level of learning the student now demonstrates high levels of competency. It is natural that a feeling of wanting to influence others now exists: the student has become the teacher and is shaping the behaviour of others — junior students, patients, relatives and other health care workers. Transfer of learning in its extrinsic form is the visible end-product of the whole learning experience.

Table 2.1   Learning principles of the experiential taxonomy (Steinaker & Bell 1979)

Taxonomic level	Teaching role	Learning principle
1 Exposure	Motivator	Extrinsic motivation Focusing Anxiety level
2 Participation	Catalyst	Initial guidance Meaning — exploration Chance for success
3 Identification	Moderator	Personal interaction Knowledge of results Reinforcement
4 Internalization	Sustainer	Overlearning Transfer (intrinsic) Differentiated input
5 Dissemination	Critic	Transfer (extrinsic) Reward Intrinsic motivation

The student's reward is the satisfaction of disseminating knowledge and skills, and influencing the values and beliefs of others. Assisting the junior student to participate in the assessment of and care planning for a patient carries with it the feeling of achievement and gratification, even though it is still a learning experience for the senior student.

The first learning principle referred to in this section was that of extrinsic or external motivation — that which would stimulate the student to want to learn. It is necessary to return to motivation to complete the account of learning principles but now the source of the drive is intrinsic, within the student, rather than an external force. The need to provide further chances for success, reinforcing, rewarding and providing knowledge of results, still exists but, by now, the student has experienced satisfaction and inner reward. The drive and desire to continue learning is now within the student and provided that opportunities are created for continuing education and professional development the motivation should be readily sustained.

The learning principles referred to are tabulated for easy reference, together with the corresponding level of learning, in Table 2.1.

Cooperative or competitive learning

When examining some of the important principles of learning, the use of terms such as motivation, chance for succes, knowledge of results and reward is inevitable; they are proven key learning factors. Many cultures in the past have instilled in their young children a spirit of competitiveness whilst at the same time attempting to impress upon the child the importance of friendship, compassion and brotherly love. Learning in some form or other appears to flourish in both sets of circumstances according to the particular individual. By that it is implied that some individuals learn some things best when there is a competitive nature to the learning environment. Other students seem to enjoy the group learning approach in which cooperation and interdependence are strong features. Which of these two attitudes to learning is best suited to the student in the practical setting? Care of patients and clients is claimed to be most effective when practised through a team approach — nurses, doctors, therapists and support staff working together to achieve a common goal. Each contributes specific skills, complementing the others. Can there be a role for the opportunist, competitor, aggressor or individualist other than that of an investor of these qualities into the team effort?

It will be argued in a later chapter that nursing education today should assume a more process-orientated approach whereby association with human activities is a strong feature, enabling the student to grow. Constant feedback and reinforcement facilitates progress, with the knowledge that objectives and competences are being achieved. Nurse teachers spend much time and energy with new intakes of student nurses helping to create group cohesion, communication and fellowship. Interpersonal skills and social interaction are given a high profile not only to enable students to relate to patients and relatives but, equally, to prompt cooperative learning and mutual support. Grading student performance leads to competitiveness which Bevis (1978) suggests is antagonistic to the process approach to learning. This is also claimed by Biehler (1971) who in addition believes that it would be unlikely for one student to help another through a particularly difficult learning activity or event. Such attitudes are reinforcers of both high and low performance. If all students are provided with learning opportunities where the probability of success is high, in which self-esteem is not threatened and where team approaches are adopted, the competitive nature of the student may become modified and learning through cooperation may feature more strongly.

Learning for keeps

Principles of learning cannot be discussed without sooner or later making reference to memory and its associated components, remembering and forgetting. Not even the most ardent supporter of experiential learning techniques can deny the significance of memory and the facility for recalling information and previous situations. However, much of the early work carried out in the field of memory, learning and study is now considered with some scepticism. Many books on the subject of educational psychology describe the forgetting curve attributed to Ebbinghaus (Fig. 2.3). Ebbinghaus (1885) committed to memory lists of three-letter nonsense words and then logged the number of words he could recall after specific periods of time.

The interpretation of this curve given by Buzan (1973) is criticised by Gibbs (1981) who claims that it is too simplistic to suggest that it applies to any situation other than the one from which it was produced. As Gibbs points out, neither the subject matter nor the method of learning bears any resemblance to academic study. Furthermore, the method Ebbinghaus used to test his memory is not one that is commonly used to assess student learning. Finally, Gibbs reminds us that a

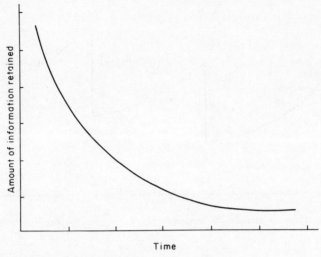

Fig. 2.3   The forgetting curve (after Ebbinghaus 1885)

substantial factor in Ebbinghaus's 'forgetting' theory, which he did not consider, can be attributed to 'interference'. This relates to the existence of memory traces of other similar features, i.e. other lists of nonsense in the case of Ebbinghaus.

Whilst not denying that facts, information and experiences are forgotten over a period of time and there are obviously indentifiable factors that can cause the forgetting process to slow down or, alternatively, accelerate it. Similarly, it is possible to develop mechanisms by which remembering can be enhanced and facilitated. Practice and revision readily spring to mind as agents of increasing remembering, particularly if carried out in a systematic manner. Buzan (1973) refers to the rehearsal of study notes after the first day, then after one week, one month, and so on. This principle of helping memory is similar to that of producing immunity to disease through vaccination and booster injections, i.e. repeated doses/study at measured intervals increase immunity/retention (Fig. 2.4).

This approach looks very attractive and no doubt can be effective, but how practical is it? Can a student so plan a learning strategy that it will enable the rehearsal of every new piece of information or allow timed repetition of experiences?

Ward sisters and other health care practitioners will need to consider the significance of these factors relating to memory, remembering and forgetting when they are involved in the supervision of students in the practical setting. How do such factors apply in this type of learning environment and what steps can the supervisor take to assist the student to retain and recall experiences and, in addition, relate them to concurrent theory?

Although learning is much more than committing to memory a series of related facts or practical activities, there are times when a sound memory and speedy

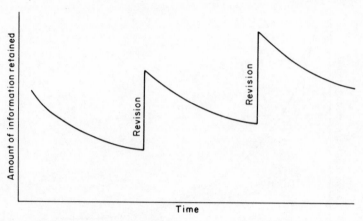

Fig. 2.4   Building up memory by revision

recall of vital information is more valuable than the highly analytical problem-solving approach. The difficulty for the student nurse is often the infrequency with which new facts or skill items are encountered. Frequency and recency are important factors in the memory process but quite often it may be the things witnessed only once that are equally easy to recall. Very few students participate more than once during their training in the procedure for the removal of a specimen of cerebrospinal fluid from a patient. Why is it that years afterwards the student recalls exactly between which lumbar vertebrae the needle was inserted and can describe the appearance, pressure and specific gravity of normal cerebrospinal fluid, and perhaps even remember Queckensted's test? There are, indeed, a number of reasons and they are applicable to most situations in which accurate retention may be desirable. Firstly, there is the 'sense of occasion', if it is the first time that the experience is to be entered into, and this is almost always an emotional as well as a cognitive learning experience. Because of these factors the student can often re-live the experience in the imagination. This second feature of memory retention, i.e. imagery, can be very intense, particularly if the emotional component of the learning happened to be particularly strong, either in a positive or negative quality. It is commonly held that circumstances involving negative emotions, i.e. fear or anger, are readily forgotten or not retained well in the memory, i.e. they are suppressed. Many qualified nurses can give very clear examples of experiences memorised for life as a result of a less-than-happy emotional situation as a student. Whilst not doubting the truth of this, one would not advocate the generation of negative emotions within the student as a means of facilitating memory retention.

Finally, in the discussion of learning principles it is appropriate to consider what responsibilities, if any, the students have towards their own learning and the development of study skills. Many enter nursing direct from secondary school or colleges of further education and will have well-established conceptions of learning and studying. It would be totally unreasonable, indeed futile, to expect students to employ new approaches to learning overnight. What it is reasonable to expect is that the student will recognise and practise new techniques of learning and begin to assume increased responsibility for self-directed study. Let us not forget that basic nurse education is primarily a vocational training into which the student has been selected, maybe through a competitive process, and in so doing has accepted that in exchange for a training allowance, a euphemism for a wage or salary, she will comply with the educational requirements of the training contract. An accompanying feature of this vocational course is that of being skills-based with an appropriate underlying theory. In the past it has been commonplace to talk about the theory and practice of nursing. This has reflected an education founded upon a knowledge base with tacked-on practice as and when available. Such courses, built on a cognitive taxonomy, are now being replaced by experiential learning models where theory is subordinate to and reflective of the 'practice' or experience. If the student is introduced to concepts of self-awareness and self-evaluation at the very beginning of the course, i.e. during the first six months, then it should be that much easier for the student to make choices about learning styles and modes of study. With a high degree of self-awareness the student can not only take on responsibility for learning but she can enhance this by fully understanding the purpose of study and the intended learning outcomes. This reflective approach to learning is a positive sign of mature student behaviour and signifies the presence of a process approach to study with which real development and progress can flourish.

References

Bevis O M (1978) *Curriculum Building in Nursing*. St Louis: Mosby
Biehler R F (1971) *Psychology Applied to Teaching*. New York: Houghton, Mifflin Company
Bloom B S (1964) *A Handbook of Educational Objectives, the Cognitive Domain*. New York: McKay
Bruner J S (1964) *Toward a Theory of Instruction*. Massachusetts: Belknap Press
Buzan T (1973) *Use your Head*. London: BBC Publications
Curzon L B (1985) *Teaching in Further Education*. New York: Holt, Rinehart & Winston
Ebbinghaus M (1885) *Uber das Gedachtmis*. Leipzig: Dunker & Humbolt
Gagne R (1983) *The Conditions of Learning*. New York: Holt, Rinehart & Winston
Gibbs G (1981) *Teaching Students to Learn*. Milton Keynes: Open University Press
Krathwohl D et al (1968) *A Handbook of Educational Objectives. The Affective Domain*. New York: McKay
Marson S (1979) Objectives, markers along the way. *Nursing Mirror*, 8 August
Maslow A H (1970) *Motivation and Personality*. New York: Harper and Row
Simpson E (1966) *The Classification of Educational Objectives. Psychomotor Domain*. Illinois: University of Illinois Press
Steinaker N W & Bell M R (1979) *The Experiential Taxonomy*. New York: Academic Press

3
The Principles of Teaching

Defining teaching

It is probable that there are as many definitions of 'teaching' as there are of 'learning' and perhaps the selection and usage of a particular definition of teaching will reflect or give clues about the teacher's own definition of learning. There are a number of words or terms that will recur in most definitions, such as 'passing on', 'communicating with', 'informing' and 'instructing': these words tend to suggest a teaching–learning relationship in which the student is a recipient, and in many cases a passive one at that. A broader description of teaching will include such terms as 'developing a new skill', 'creating awareness', and activities which 'enable', 'facilitate', 'motivate' and 'promote'. This suggests a more active relationship between student and teacher.

Teaching is traditionally perceived as a planned, structured activity based upon certain goals, aims and objectives designed to bring about some increase or improvement in a student's knowledge of a subject. This does not deny the fact that learning takes place in the absence of planned teaching or, indeed, deny that learning takes place in the absence of any sort of teaching, planned or unplanned. This chapter is almost exclusively concerned with how the qualified nurse, midwife or health visitor functions as a teacher in the caring environment. A significant feature of this teaching and learning relationship is that both teacher and student are fulfilling mutliple roles. Furthermore, it is important to recognise that the student is both an adult and a willing participant in an educational process.

The student nurse probably considers herself primarily as a nurse and secondarily as a student. A substantial amount of course time is spent with patients or clients, with the student contributing to direct care-giving. In addition to supervising and teaching student nurses the qualified nurse is a planner, implementer and evaluator of care. Because the student is both an adult and a willing learner it should be possible for the teaching in the practical setting to follow a distinct andragogical approach (this is in contrast to pedagogy which relates primarily to the science of teaching children). A wholly different set of values and beliefs is required when teaching adults, not the least of which is the emphasis on the processes of learning rather than on product or content.

Teaching as applied to the andragogy theory is concerned with the creation of positive learning environments and provision of effective learning opportunities. Didactic instruction and exposition has very little relevance or utility in this educational climate. In the previous chapter a definition of learning offered by Curzon (1985) was preferred to the more pedagogical description and, similarly with teaching, Curzon's definition would seem to be entirely compatible with the ethos of nursing education. He suggests that teaching should be considered as the deliberate and systematic creation and control of the conditions in which learning does occur.

The teacher's role in clinical practice

Qualified nurses in clinical practice are reticent about adopting the title of teacher, yet when asked to describe their job the terms 'supervising students' or 'having students on the ward' would feature strongly. Halsbury (1974) recommended that ward sisters' salaries should reflect their roles as teachers and assessors of student nurses. Consider the potential educational or training activities that an experienced nurse could be involved with:

— member of curriculum development team
— member of examination board
— ward-based assessor/examiner
— production of ward learning objectives
— preparation of student progress reports
— completion of course evaluation reports
— implementing ward teaching programmes
— teaching and assessing role development

It is probably easier to describe what is not required of the teacher in the clinical setting than to try to analyse the practical teaching role. Any attempt to recreate a classroom environment must be avoided. The ward sister who asks the senior tutor if the school has a blackboard that is no longer used and whether she could have it fixed to the office or clinic room wall in order to enable to teach the student is surely now an anachronism. Whilst it is valuable for a hospital ward to have a few nursing and medical books for reference purposes, setting a student a chapter to read during visiting time on which she will be 'tested' before going off-duty can no longer be accepted as good educational practice. Perhaps these examples of 'bad teaching' are an exaggeration but they nevertheless serve to make a point.

A growing concern among many nurse educationists is not who is the ideal person to teach within the practical setting but who is the only credible and professionally acceptable person to teach nursing at the patient/client level: increasingly, the response to this question has to be the competent nurse practitioner, i.e. the practising nurse. No matter how well intentioned, well prepared and well motivated are nurse teachers and clinical teachers to extend their teaching role to the bedside, they can only be second best to the ward sister or experienced staff nurse who has planned, implemented and evaluated the care of the patients and who is professionally accountable for that care. From the logistic point of view, there are competent nurses on all wards, in all departments and practising in the community, yet there is probably one nurse teacher to every twenty students who are spread across a number of areas of practice. How futile it seems to be to expect the nurse teacher to carry her teaching skills into the practice setting when viewed from this perspective – how much simpler and more appropriate to provide each qualified nurse with the opportunity to acquire skills in teaching and assessing.

Over the years there have been numerous and varied approaches to preparing mainly the ward sister to fulfil her responsibilities towards nurse education and the student. These have ranged from three-day art of examining courses to more sophisticated attempts to provide the ward sister with some teaching skills. Many health authorities have acknowledged the worth of courses such as the City and Guilds Course 730, Further Education Teacher's Certificate, and assisted staff to attend local colleges on a day-release basis. A few schools of nursing have actually brought the City and Guilds Course 730 in-house, either in collaboration with the local college or independently. Many authorities have done little or nothing to prepare nursing staff for their teaching role. The E N B Course 998 is the first nationally validated course expressly designed to meet this specific need. Finally, when making the strong claim that the practising nurse is the most appropriate and credible person to fulfil the clinical teaching role, it must be added that health authorities, have, of course, to find the resources to fund this activity. It may well be that in future only those authorities who are willing and able to prepare their 'practical teachers' adequately will receive the statutory approval to run basic nurse education courses.

Subsequent chapters deal very specifically with the teaching methodology, describing such terms as role model, mentor and facilitator.

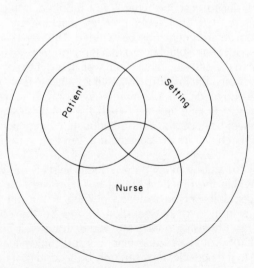

Fig. 3.1   A conceptual model of nursing (Chater 1979)

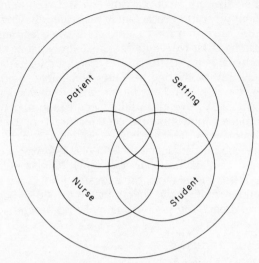

Fig. 3.2   A conceptual model of practical nurse teaching

A very simple conceptual model of nursing was described by Chater (1979) showing three interlocking circles which represent the patient or client, the nurse and the environment or setting in which care is given (Fig. 3.1). Adding a fourth interlocking circle representing the student would seem to provide a very apt conceptual model of practical nurse teaching (Fig. 3.2).

This conceptual model clearly suggests that nurse, patient and student have a relationship which is interactional and, therefore, interpersonal, with each party having roles and responsibilities as well as needs and expectations. The balance and emphasis of these aspects differ, of course, between the participants, but each has something to give and receive from the others.

The concept of an experiential curriculum has already been advanced when learning principles were described. Applying the same five stages of the experiential taxonomy to teaching roles and strategies that were applied to learning principles makes it possible to match appropriate teaching approaches with student learning needs. This seems particularly relevant in the practical teaching and learning setting where students are participating in realistic experiences.

The nurse supervisor as motivator

The first level of the experiential learning process is characterised by the student being exposed to the subject of the learning situation. Accompanying this level of learning are the principles of external motivation, focusing and management of anxiety. The corresponding teaching role is that of motivator. For a student nurse in the initial stages of the course it is essential that supervision by the qualified nurse should provide not only opportunities to learn but also safe ones — total protection so that anxiety levels are not such that they interfere with learning in a negative way. Perhaps for the teacher in the clinical setting being a motivator for the student at the exposure level of learning is not very much of a problem. Clearly, the student nurse is already highly motivated: having competed for a place on the course she is only too eager to commence learning in the reality of the patient environment. However, three years, plus, is a long time in the life of a young adult and initial enthusiasm tends to wane sooner or later. It is at these times that the skill of remotivating becomes invaluable. Being able to create within the student the desire and need to progress from one level of learning to another is not always easy. An early positive, secure rapport between the student and supervisor is necessary without the need for threats or excessive demands. Well-directed observations, together with realistic demonstration and problem identification, may help to stimulate the student. Knowing that a student has particular strengths can be useful to the supervising nurse when planning learning opportunities. It is vital that the exposure level of learning is managed well in terms of student motivation. Unless there is a desire to begin to participate in the learning experience the student will make no progress.

The nurse supervisor as catalyst

The word 'catalyst' sounds very scientific and complex yet it is the only meaningful word to describe the role of the nurse at this level of student learning. The purpose or aim is to assist the process of change along the learning continuum, i.e. from observation of an experience or activity to participation in it. In chemical terms, a catalyst is a change facilitator that speeds up a reaction between two or more substances. Using this analogy the teacher, together with appropriate resources, enables a change to take place between the student and the object of the learning experience. This provides the student with an opportunity to develop not only an intellectual commitment or understanding but also an emotional attachment. During this transitional period the practical teacher must maintain a good level of motivation in the student and protect her from the risk of failure. Close supervision, prompting where necessary and at all times keeping the student well informed about the 'what, 'why' and 'how' of the nursing activity are characteristics of an effective role model. If the teacher fails to act as a catalyst at this participation level of the learning process many things could happen, which may not only slow learning down but even prevent learning from taking place. A student who is told to obtain a specimen of urine from a patient and is shown how to test the specific gravity but is not given any explanation of why it has to be done does not have the total picture; a part of the experience is missing and with it the potential for developing that growing commitment upon which the next stage of the learning process depends. Equally as bad is the situation in which a student is given a full explanation of why a nursing activity is to be carried out but is inadequately prepared for or supervised in its execution. This situation is potentially dangerous. A bad experience for the student at this stage can bring a complete halt to the learning process. As with the previous level of learning where the teacher took on the role of motivator, the catalyst function is of an extrinsic nature. The student has a somewhat passive role still and is even being manipulated in many of the learning situations. Through repeated participation in well-planned activities, however, the student will become both intellectually and emotionally attached to the experience, and at this stage the teacher's role will need to change again.

The nurse supervisor as moderator

In simple terms, a moderator is someone who sees that things are kept within certain limits, preventing extremes from occurring or being brought to bear on a situation. The student is now at the stage of learning where 'ownership' of the skills, activity or experience is claimed. Identification of the learning experience has taken place and the student is incorporating the new learning into professional behaviour. During this identification level the student will seek to test newly acquired skills. Will they 'work' in differing circumstances with different patients? It is at times like this when the student, not yet experienced, wants to experiment that the supervisor has to ensure 'moderation' in practice.

Although the nurse supervisor is now playing a more passive role, it is essential that the learning opportunities should be available and provide a meaningful sequence of experiences for the student. Positive reinforcement must be given and the role model is consistently questioning and suggesting appropriate student actions, clarifying any problem areas as they occur.

Some qualified nurse supervisors may find this particular role difficult to come to terms with. They are being urged to teach student nurses yet at significant stages in the learning process a passive role is recommended. This is understandable because of the traditional concepts of the teaching role, yet at this level the teacher is manipulating the student through a learning experience and controlling the learning environment.

Sensitive handling of the student is called for, assisting with such interactive needs as she may have in terms of sharing the positive experiences and receiving appropriate feedback. These new behaviours, which the student demonstrates and develops a commitment for, are now becoming assimilated into the growing repertoire of acquired skills. The teacher will assist by helping with the selection of relevant information and its use, giving the student regular indications of progress and achievement.

The nurse supervisor as sustainer

The level of learning for which the particular teaching role is best suited is that of internalisation. Having identified with a particular skill or nursing activity and 'tested' it in a variety of situations it can now be reproduced without any conscious effort. The skill has become a learned behaviour for the student, a permanent feature of the range of necessary competences that will lead to qualification. As with the previous level of learning, the teaching role is relatively passive: much support is still necessary as the student requires constant approval, particularly where recently acquired skills are being used in new situations. It is important that she should recognise the appropriateness of the action and see it as a positive contribution to the care of the patient/client.

A word of caution may be necessary at this point. Where very specific behavioural objectives have been prepared for students there could be some variation in initial performance: the degree of motivation, the student's own interpretation and the different response levels will influence the learning outcomes. Provided these responses are within acceptable parameters the nurse supervisor can engineer necessary adjustments. An important feature of the sustainer role is the requirement to provide the student with additional scope for practice, extending her experience and enabling the transference of skills. Perhaps rather than manipulating the student the nurse supervisor is adjusting the learning environment, creating different learning opportunities. New experiences can seriously challenge the student, stretching her ability to adapt and adjust. As a sustainer of learning, the teacher will be remotivating whenever necessary, promoting creativity and encouraging innovation, and yet remain sensitive to all the demands being made upon the student.

The nurse supervisor as critic

At the beginning of this account of the different roles of the nurse supervisor in relation to the student's level of learning it was evident that the teacher adopted an active stance. This gradually became more passive as the student progressed along the learning continuum. Such a shift in emphasis within the teacher–student relationship is common, particularly in further and higher education. The statutory bodies for nursing in recent years have advocated a curriculum strategy whereby initial teacher-directed approaches gradually give way to student-

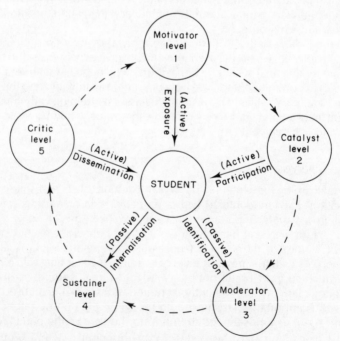

Fig. 3.3   Teaching roles in relation to levels of learning

centred learning and, eventually, to self-directed study. This model would appear to be completely appropriate to adult learning until the question of the student moving on to a new learning experience occurs. Because at this stage self-directed learning is the mode, are new learning activities left to chance or should the teacher assume an active role again? In the model being offered here the highest level of learning, described as dissemination, is accompanied by a teaching role that places the nurse supervisor firmly back into an active position relative to the student. The nurse supervisor is now a critic, appraising, evaluating and advising the student. With objective criticism and by asking questions or posing further problems the teacher prepares the way for new learning experiences. This model is more cyclical, in that the highest level of learning is often the precursor of new experiences, and this time the motivation to learn may be intrinsic rather than the extrinsic provision via the teacher.

This sequence of teacher roles in relation to the levels of learning within an experience is, of course, a model or framework for the teacher, and it is readily acknowledged that roles may need to change or undergo modification within the prevailing circumstances. A simple representation of the model is shown in Fig. 3.3.

The curriculum process in the practical setting

Until recently, all basic nursing courses have been founded upon a syllabus published by the statutory body. Although this still applies in mental illness and mental handicap nursing courses, i.e. the 1982 Syllabus, courses currently being approved in general nursing do not have a syllabus as a base or foundation. Project 2000 (U K C C 1986) notes amongst recent major changes in nurse education the shift away from prescribing the exact knowledge to be obtained. This move is concerned with devolving responsibility of curriculum process to the individual schools and giving support and advice through the use of guidelines and general principles. The syllabus for courses leading to registration in Part 1 of the Professional Register (general nursing) was formally withdrawn by the English National Board in 1986 (Circular 1986/65/E R D B). It was replaced by guidelines published in the previous year (Circular 1985/19/E R D B) to assist schools of nursing in the design and development of curricula to meet the requirements of Rule 18(1) of the Nurses, Midwives and Health Visitors Rules Approval Order 1983 (D H S S 1983): this rule is reproduced in Table 3.1. The licence and flexibility permitted by the statutory bodies for selecting teaching and learning strategies by which the 'product' can be achieved is welcome; however, it can make demands upon curriculum designers and the students' supervisors.

As previously implied, practical nurses must be well represented on the curriculum design and development team. They must examine and become familiar with all aspects of the course and not just the unit or that part of the programme in which they are personally involved. The progression of the student nurse from day one of the course is planned in a sequential manner, and different learning and teaching principles are required which are dependent upon the stage of the student's development within the course. Not all competences

Table 3.1   United Kingdom Central Council training rules (Nurses, Midwives and Health Visitors Rules Approval Order 1983, Cmd 873)

18(1) Courses leading to a qualification the successful completion of which shall enable an application to be made for admission to Part 1 of the register shall provide opportunities to enable the student to accept responsibility for her personal professional development and to acquire the competencies required to:

(a)   advise on the promotion of health and the prevention of illness;
(b)   recognise situations that may be detrimental to the health and well-being of the individual;
(c)   carry out those activities involved when conducting the comprehensive assessment of a person's nursing requirements;
(d)   recognise the significance of the observations made and use these to develop an initial nursing assessment;
(e)   devise a plan of nursing care based on the assessment with the co-operation of the patient, to the extent that this is possible, taking into account the medical prescription;
(f)   implement the planned programme of nursing care and where appropriate teach and co-ordinate other members of the caring team who may be responsible for implementing specific aspects of the nursing care;
(g)   review the effectiveness of the nursing care provided, and where appropriate, initiate any action that may be required;
(h)   work in a team with other nurses, and with medical and paramedical staff and social workers;
(i)   undertake the management of the care of a group of patients over a period of time and organise the appropriate support services;

related to the care of the particular type of patient with whom she is likely to come in contact when registered in that Part of the register for which the student intends to qualify.

will be attained at the same rate; some will be achieved relatively early in the course, i.e. health promotion, whilst those relating to teaching and management will be acquired nearer the end of the course. Because of the very real potential for causing confusion and misunderstanding in the nurse supervisor, it is vital that the curriculum design team should, in consultation with the nurse supervisors, devise appropriate teaching strategies for each unit of practical experience and the concurrent theory to that experience. This will usually take the form of written objectives designed to enable the student to achieve a goal or aim for that part of the course. When put into the form of questions to be answered, the nurse supervisor needs to know the following:

—   What purpose or purposes should be achieved by the student in the particular practical placement?
—   What experiences can be provided to enable the purposes to be achieved?
—   How can these experiences be effectively prepared and arranged?
—   How can the attainment of these purposes be measured?

These questions are still as relevant today as they were almost forty years ago when referred to in Tyler's (1949) work on curriculum development. Childs (1985) comments on Tyler's use of the word 'experience' instead of 'content', reflecting that the term 'experience' not only concerns the subject material taught but the process by which the learning takes place. Childs summarises the four questions posed by Tyler as: objectives, content, method and evaluation.

Objectives

At the practical experience level, an objective can be defined as a statement describing what the student nurse will be able to do after completing the practical placement: it is a comparison of the behaviour of the student after the learning experience with that before it. Because of this reference to behaviour, these objectives are more commonly referred to as behavioural objectives.

When describing objectives, Curzon (1985) differentiates between the general objective and the specific objective. The general objective is sometimes referred to as the terminal objective because it states the behaviour expected at the end of a unit of learning or a practical placement. Similarly, the specific objectives may be described as developmental objectives because they are achieved during the course unit and their sum total results in the achievement of the terminal objective. Some advocates of behavioural objectives will be even more specific in describing the expected behaviours. In addition to a description of the observable behaviour, the teacher may state the conditions under which the behaviour is to be achieved and, furthermore, the precise criteria for successful attainment. Translated into nursing practice, a behavioural objective concerning the administration of drugs may look like this:

On completion of this learning exercise the student will be able to:
(a)   carry out a ward medicine round
(b)   under the supervision of a qualified nurse
(c)   and in accordance with the authority's policy.

Just as there are advocates of this approach to learning and the rigid setting of objectives there are those who severely criticise behaviourism in any shape or form. They argue that to specify predetermined outcomes to all learning situations is more akin to training, whereas education, whilst not denying the end-product, is just as much concerned with the process by which the product is achieved. What nurses have to decide is whether nursing is a profession or a vocation. If it is the latter, then perhaps training with behavioural objectives is an appropriate learning approach. In the practical nursing setting the wide diversity of learning opportunities, combined with the complexity of individual differences in patients or clients, would seem to render the construction of strict behavioural objectives expensive of time and effort. The number of behavioural statements that could be involved might be too numerous to cope with. Nor do behavioural objectives take into account the uniqueness of the individual student and the previous experiences undergone.

The experiential approach to curriculum design and process, whilst acknowledging the necessity of objectives, links them to the broader experience rather than to a narrow behavioural outcome. This allows for, and indeed encourages, the individuality of the student, recognising that learning speeds, motivation, special interests and expectations vary widely amongst course members even where there is a common goal or purpose. Perhaps in such a diverse subject as nursing there is room for both behavioural and experiential objectives. The emergency situation which threatens life requires the nurse to be very specific in her behaviour towards the patient; a skill learned through very precise behavioural objectives. The building up of a supportive and therapeutic relationship with a newly bereaved relative can perhaps be achieved very rarely when using behavioural learning objectives.

There is no denying that teaching and learning objectives of some form or other help to bring some structure to most types of educational course, providing a framework upon which teaching strategies and assessment criteria can be based. At the practical level in the clinical setting, the qualified nurse who fulfills the supervisory role in basic nurse education must play a prominent part in the formulation of objectives. These objectives must be realistic, meaningful and truly reflect the care practices taking place: it is futile for theoreticians to design ideal objectives that bear no relationship to the practical reality in which the student is required to gain experience.

It may be helpful at this stage to provide the reader with specific examples of different types of objectives as they might appear in the curriculum structure of a basic nursing course (Fig. 3.4).

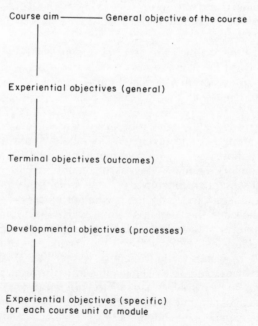

Fig. 3.4   Curriculum model showing sequence of objectives

The course aim

To produce a contemporary nurse who can respond to consumer demands and needs using problem-solving techniques that reflect a wide range of technical, behavioural and intellectual skills.

General objectives of the course

The course will provide opportunities to enable the student to acquire the competences specified by Rule 18(1) of the Nurses, Midwives and Health Visitors Rules Approval Order 1983 (Cmd 873) (Table 3.1).

Experiential objectives (general)

The course will expose the student to nursing practices using appropriate role models who reflect nursing competency:

— The course will enable the student to participate in experiences with competent role models in the giving of total patient care.
— The course will encourage the student to identify with competent care-giving as practised by the role model.
— The course will enable the student to internalise the skills of a competent nurse.
— The course will prepare the student to disseminate the competences described in Rule 18(1) (Table 3.1).

Terminal objectives (outcomes)

— The student will be able to accept responsibility for personal professional development.
— The student will advise on the promotion of health and prevention of illness.
— The student will recognise situations that are detrimental to health and well-being.
— The student will be able to assess a patient's nursing requirements.
— The student will devise nursing care plans, with the patient's cooperation where possible.
— The student will implement planned care and teach other care team members whilst coordinating their activities.
— The student will review and evaluate care given to patients.
— The student will work effectively in a multidisciplinary team setting.
— The student will manage the care of patients, organising appropriate support services.

Development objectives (processes)

— The student will demonstrate an understanding of situations detrimental to physical, emotional and social well-being and will show a responsibility towards the promotion of health.

— The student will demonstrate an ability to give total nursing care to a specific patient whilst under the supervision of a qualified nurse.
— The student will develop this ability and be able to assume responsibility for the nursing care given.
— The student will become competent in implementing and evaluating nursing care for a group of patients.
— The student will develop the ability to manage the total care of a group of patients.
— The student will consistently demonstrate the nursing competencies described by Rule 18(1) (Table 3.1).

Experiential objectives (specific to a course unit)

When designing objectives for a particular part of a course, it would appear desirable to write these in terms of nursing behaviours and, wherever possible, associated with one or more of the nursing competencies of Rule 18(1) (Table 3.1). The following are examples of such experiential objectives taken from an early course unit of a basic student general nursing course.

Exposure level   'The student has observed the qualified nurse's use of the skills of listening, responding and clinical observation which are needed to complete a patient assessment.

This first level of learning, i.e. exposure to an experience, in this example is linked with the competencies (c) and (d) of Rule 18(1).

Participation level   'The student has participated in the planning of nursing care under the supervision of a qualified nurse.'

In this example the student has progressed to the second level of learning, i.e. participation, and competency (e) of Rule 18(1) is the focus of study.

Identification level   'The student demonstrates an awareness that many situations in health care provision may be detrimental to the individual's health.'

This objective, pitched at the third level of experiential learning, is concerned with competency (b) of Rule 18(1) and requires the student to have developed an understanding of health hazards, institutional problems and safety risks when caring for patients and their relatives.

Internalisation level   'The student can explain the purpose of care given and its relation to the level of dependency of the patient.'

The student who has 'internalised' a particular experience has incorporated the required skills into the nursing behaviour. In this example, competency (f) of Rule 18(1) provides the basis for the learning objective.

Dissemination level   'The student can advise the patient and relatives on matters of health promotion by acting as a role model.'

At this highest level of learning the student can be observed to be 'teaching' others about their experiences and demonstrating skill in their professional behaviour. The objective given here relates to competency (a) of Rule 18(1).

Course content at the practical level

Having defined the teaching and learning objectives for the course as a whole and for each of its component parts, the next stage in the curriculum process centres on the selection or identification of appropriate experiences and subject content. For the nurse supervisor in the clinical setting this will very much depend upon two things: firstly, the objectives that the student must achieve in relation to the stage of training, i.e. first year, second year, third year, and, secondly, the nature or discipline of the experience, i.e. medical, orthopaedic, psychiatric, and so on.

In a curriculum that is substantially skills-based, the knowledge or theory components are secondary to and supportive of those skills required to achieve the objectives of a course unit. The qualified nurse who is charged with the supervision of student nurses will need to give attention to questions such as:

— What is the student to learn?
— How is it to be learned?
— Why is it being learned?
— How much attention must be given to it?

These questions relating to curricular process are by no means complicated or profound but until recently it is unlikely that many qualified nurse supervisors would have been required to provide answers to them. Perhaps a cardinal rule for all teachers at the practical level is to present material or information to a student only in such a way that it has to be used or acted upon immediately (Bevis 1978).

What the qualified nurse supervisor must resist at all costs is the temptation to teach 'pet' subjects to the student. There is no point in a student nurse being able to recite the names and functions of the twelve pairs of cranial nerves whilst gaining practical experience in the community with patients requiring mental health care.

Concurrent theory and practice is advocated by the statutory body and this should be interpreted as the provision of background information and knowledge to support the practical experiences as they occur or are managed. The situation in which a student is denied the experience of accompanying a patient who is to undergo a liver biopsy because the anatomy and physiology of the liver has not been taught in the school should not occur. As a student receives new experiences in the clinical setting, she should be prompted and guided to acquire the relevant support material and information so that a total meaning is obtained for that experience and it can form a link in the educational chain. Accepting that some of the experiences and the associated knowledge will be specialised, the nurse supervisor should, nevertheless, give significant emphasis to the core topics. These may differ slightly depending upon the course but ought to revolve around such themes as health concepts, care models, the nursing process and personal service.

Teaching strategies (method)

Learning principles were considered in the previous chapter and teacher roles were looked at in the earlier part of this one. Probably the most important feature of the curriculum process is the teaching strategies, and these cannot be discussed in isolation. It is the amalgam of learning principles, teacher roles and teaching strategies that sets the scene for the teacher–student relationship and with it the whole teaching–learning process. All too often a curriculum is prepared with detailed attention to learning objectives and subject content and is then handed over to the teacher without any attempt being made to suggest appropriate teaching strategies. Whilst this is unfortunate if it happens to the professional teacher, it must be considered inexcusable and totally unacceptable for the nurse supervisor to be placed in such a situation.

Fortunately, when using the experiential approach to teaching and learning this should rarely happen. The teaching strategies considered appropriate at each level of learning are proposed in association with the learning principles, and simultaneously the role of the teacher in the teaching–learning activity is suggested. Nevertheless, as Kelly (1982) warns, it is the teacher, in this case the nurse supervisor, who has the task of bridging the final gap which might exist between theory and practice. Ideally, all teachers and supervisors who are to participate in curiculum implementation should have been involved in its design. This can be partially achieved when designing nursing courses by involving clinically based nurses who are to be the supervisors of students in the appropriate stage of course design. Two purposes can be achieved in doing this: firstly, by contributing directly to course design the nurse identifies with the course and becomes involved with its ownership and, secondly, the role-specific needs of nurse supervisors can usually be revealed at this juncture and the necessary development training and role preparation planned.

The description of teaching strategies may be better understood if they are considered in the context of nursing themes, i.e. care models, nursing process and health concept. It will also be necessary for the reader to recall the table of learning principles in the previous chapter. Just as certain principles are found to be appropriate to particular learning levels so, too, are specific teaching strategies. Such strategies are now described using the levels of learning as the sequence for presentation. The activities of the living model described by Roper et al (1983) will be used as the example of a nursing approach, mainly because it appears to be the commonest model being used in the United Kingdom health service.

Teaching strategies at exposure level

Goal setting   The nurse supervisor will introduce the concept of daily activities of living to the student and endeavour to create an incentive within the student to explore the concept in detail.

Data presentation   Using the student's own experiences of daily living a profile or checklist of activities can be developed.

Demonstration   Some of the underlying principles of daily living activities can be demonstrated by the supervisor using examples of patients behaviour, students' own behaviour or media resource material.

Directed observation   Selecting a number of activities of living, e.g. eating, breathing, personal cleanliness, etc., the student can analyse in detail how an activity is carried out.

Data exploration   The student should now follow up the analysis by interpreting findings and extracting relevant information for care planning purposes.

These five teaching strategies are designed to shape the students' observational skills and become more aware of their own experiences of living whilst examining the life processes of other people.

Teaching strategies at participation level

Recall   As part of the preparation for participation the student should review the information acquired at exposure level. Comparison of one's own needs for fulfilling activities of living and independence with those of patients will help in understanding the dependence–independence continuum.

Expanding information   The information gathered can now be expanded through discussion with the supervisor or peers in such a way that experiences are shared. Questions can be asked relating to the identification of resources needed to meet the dependency needs of patients and plans for helping patients to fulfil their activities of living can be proposed, formulated and examined.

Role-play   Although this teaching strategy is usually more appropriate to the classroom, it may have occasional use in the practical experience setting. The supervisor may wish to rehearse with the student such activities as patient admission, interviews, counselling and other interactive processes. Role-play may prove to be the best preparatory method, provided the rehearsal is not too artificial or unreal.

Practice participation   Supervised practice can now follow in the reality of the patient setting and basic nursing activities carried out working alongside an experienced role model. In addition to the physical manipulation skills, the student must be encouraged to practise observational and communication skills.

Ordering   Following participation in assessing, planning and implementing basic care designed to assist patients with activities of living, the student should now analyse the particular role played. Additional information will have been collected in transit and mistakes will have been made. This information can now be arranged, sequenced and structured into a planned framework for future practice.

Teaching strategies at identification level

Active participation   The student should now be ready for more sustained practice whilst still under the supervision of a nurse. Although experience is now being gained with all components of the nursing process emphasis for the student will still be around the application of caring skills.

Using information   It should now become apparent to the student that existing information can no longer meet the diversity of caring situations being experienced. Additional reading will be necessary and the student will begin to use information and interpret it to meet new circumstances. Patients have different degrees of dependence and need: some are keen to participate in self-help, others enjoy being dependent. Increased skills of observation and communication will enable the student to use information more effectively. This principle is well supported by Taylor (1985) who suggests that the skill of information processing should be acquired at an early stage in training in order to facilitate the use of new content and assist the student in the analysis of new data.

Interactive discussion   Opportunity must be provided by the supervisor during the allocation to practical experience for the student to discuss future expectations and anticipated progression. It is important for the student to be able to express ideas, discuss new information and review outcomes of practice. During ward meetings discussion designed to clarify problem areas, identify difficulties and allow expression of opinions will help with the reinforcement of learning. Debate can be centred around some of the less physical aspects of living, e.g. expressing sexuality, assisting patients to communicate and caring for the dying. The student will need some feedback on the achievement of progress and the supervisor can use this interactive discussion to advise the student of weaknesses and, equally important, reinforce strengths.

Hypothesising   As the student's skills and confidence increase so will the ability to ask questions in relation to the carrying out of care. 'When I discussed my particular interest in painting with Mrs Green she said it was also her main hobby and she has now expressed an interest to do some painting in the evenings when the ward is quiet.' 'I wonder if I can discover Mrs Brown's hobbies or interests and encourage her to participate in something creative or diversional?'

The student is now beginning to examine in depth the activities of living and see connections between meeting these and the promotion of independence. Assumptions based upon reasoning are now being produced.

Before proceeding to the teaching strategies appropriate to the higher levels of learning it is necessary to do a quick stock-take of the progress made along the teaching–learning continuum. The student has by now undergone a substantial period of practical experience, participating in the nursing care of patients whilst using a particular model of care. During this time the student will have gathered, analysed and acted upon a wide range of information. Ideas will have been generated and tested against reality under the supervision of a competent role model, and degrees of success will have been experienced. The student should now be able to demonstrate an understanding of the 'activities of living' approach to care and how it is implemented using the nursing process. It is important that not only does the student understand the model of care but is able to appreciate that many other models of nursing exist.

Teaching strategies at internalisation level

Skill reinforcement As the student progresses through the course, gaining experience with different patient or client groups in different clinical settings, existing skills will be tested in new settings and reinforcement of the more productive elements of care will take place.

Creative expression Just as theoretical knowledge can be enhanced by providing an opportunity for practical application so, too, can skills be strengthened, enriched and reinforced by encouraging the student to write about experiences and talk to others about them in a group or seminar. By doing this the student is giving expression to internalised learning and sharing both with peers and supervisors. Being able to talk about experiences adds a further dimension to the learning and is valuable preparation for transition to the dissemination level.

Role-play and simulation The testing of skills amongst peers can be further extended by the use of role-play and simulation. Because the student is now both emotionally and intellectually committed to the concept of nursing models and health promotion, the use of advanced role-play can enable full expression and interpretation of these concepts. The student can gain practice in developing the role of health educator by trying out a range of health promotion strategies in the safety and security of her supervisor's protection. It is equally important for the student to appreciate and understand the consumer's feelings and point of view as a receiver of health education and nursing practices. With the use of simulation the student can stand in the patient role whilst a peer or supervisor plays the role of health promoter. Role-play is an effective expression of internalised learning, whilst simulation is an expression of understanding and therefore probably less threatening for the student. Internalised behaviour during simulation can be allowed expression without risk of ego-damage.

Comparative analysis Although the student has by now experienced a number of different patient settings in which to carry out nursing care, these experiences will probably have had a degree of similarity in that they may all have taken place within a particular type of hospital setting. Can the student utilise her nursing skills in a totally different environment with a very different patient/client group? How will the student adjust and modify the approach to an acutely mentally ill patient in the psychiatric unit or to a domineering ex-patient in his own home? Such situations will test the student's critical thinking and problem-solving abilities. The nurse may have achieved the skills of meeting the personal hygiene needs of a helpless patient confined to bed but will the same techniques succeed with a severely depressed suicidal patient? This difference in the type of experience enables the student to compare and contrast the utility of the nursing model and how the nursing role has to change in approach and application. The student will need to analyse critically the similarity and differences that a new client group or care environment creates, and with the help of a skilful role model broaden the knowledge base and add to the repertoire of skills.

Summarising   The internalisation of the activities of a living model is almost complete. Because learning sequences have been well planned and learning has taken place by intent rather than by accident, the student can possibly review the process that has been undertaken. Any activity that helps the student to summarise or conclude the whole concept of activities of living will be most helpful in rounding off the internalisation end of learning. The presentation of a seminar paper to the ward team or the submission of a written assignment to the supervisor would serve this purpose.

Teaching strategies at dissemination level

Reporting   Dissemination is totally a student-centred activity: it cannot be demanded by a supervisor or, more accurately, it should not be demanded. The student having internalised the competences of carrying out total patient care is, on comparative terms, an 'authority' on the subject. Not only should the student wish to share experiences with others but should be positive in advocating them to nursing colleagues. Additionally, the student at this level should be willing to defend her work and deal confidently with objective criticisms.

Oral presentation   As the student's desire to advocate her learning to others grows, not only will opportunities be used as they arise but the student will seek to create opportunities. Whilst carrying out nursing activities with patients, the student may offer health-promoting advice with regard to diet, exercise and smoking. Similarly with relatives, the student may tactfully introduce health concepts into the general conversation. Although these two activities would appear to be very similar there is a distinct difference in emphasis: with the patient the nurse will be seeking to change behaviour whereas with relatives the emphasis is usually more informational than prescriptive.

Dramatisation, group discussion, seminar   In addition to written reports and oral presentations there are a number of dissemination strategies available to the student. Many situations of a social or psychological nature lend themselves to dramatisation, particularly in areas where a health education message is desired. Dramatisation differs from role-play in that the student creates a theme and writes the script which is then acted before an audience. Although this has limited use as a teaching strategy in the clinical setting, the nurse supervisor may wish to utilise it in health education activities for patients and relatives.

Group discussion at ward meetings and seminar presentation to team members are social activities in which the student can participate. Through debate, an attempt can be made to influence others and also to test beliefs and values against the opinions of others. Seminar or group discussions may give rise to new ideas and extensions to concepts that have previously eluded the care team.

In concluding the description of teaching strategies, it must be emphasised that rarely do students complete the five levels of learning in one course unit. For

Table 3.2 Summary of learning and teaching strategies (After Steinaker & Bell 1979)

Taxonomic level	Learning principles	Teaching strategies	Teacher role

1 Exposure	Extrinsic motivation
	Focusing
	Anxiety level
		Goal-setting
		  motivation
		  presentation
		Demonstration
		Directed
		  observation
		Data exploration
			Motivator
			Information

2 Participation	Initial guidance
	Meaning —
	  exploration
	Chance for success
		Recall
		Expanding
		  information base
		Role-play
		Practice
		  participation
		Ordering
			Catalyst

3 Identification	Personal
	  interaction
	Knowledge of
	  results
	Reinforcement
		Active
		  participation
		Using information
		Interactive
		  discussion
		Hypothesising
		Testing
			Moderator

4 Internalization	Overlearning
	Transfer (intrinsic)
	Differentiated
	  input
		Skill reinforcement
		Creative expression
		Role-play —
		  simulation
		Comparative
		  analysis
		Summarization
			Sustainer

5 Dissemination	Transfer (extrinsic) Reward Motivation (instrinsic)	Reporting Oral presentation Dramatisation Group dynamics Seminar	Critic

some of the more complex concepts an entire course is needed to enable the student to progress from exposure to dissemination and competency. A summary of the teaching strategies relative to the levels and principles of learning is given in Table 3.2.

Assessment within the teaching strategies

Although specific chapters (4 and 5) are devoted to the subject of assessment, it is necessary here to say a few words about the practical nurse and the assessment function in relation to the teacher strategies that have just been described.

Assessment at the exposure level of learning

At this first level of learning, the nurse supervisor provides learning experiences designed to stimulate the student's interest with a view to motivating her to seek further exposure to the experience and begin to interact with it. Assessment involves observing the student and judging her levels of interest and interaction. It may be possible even at this early stage to assess initial understanding and attitudes towards the experience. Informal methods such as ward team discussions, question and answer, and nurse supervisor observations are appropriate during this learning stage.

Assessment at the participation level of learning

Participation implies a conscious decision by the student to become involved in the learning experience. Again, observation by the nurse supervisor is an obvious assessment method provided it is acknowledged that at this stage much of the learning may not be overtly expressed. To reveal covert learning the supervisor would need constantly to question the student to determine levels of learning, and this is neither practical nor desirable. A better approach would be to vary the learning opportunities so that students can make choices and interact with a number of alternative situations, thereby revealing more overtly a comprehension of their participation.

Assessment at the identification learning level

Identification with the learning experience is achieved when the student begins to convert the satisfaction of participatory achievement into intellectual commitment. At this level there is a tendency for overt expression of the learning, the student often wishing to share her learning with others. Assessment at this stage must be used to reinforce learning and reveal to the student some degree of achievement, and it must also identify attainment of goals in the form of unit objectives. Assignments, surveys and projects are most probably the methods of choice because their outcomes can be used in a formative way and, additionally, they can be criterion-referenced.

Assessment at the internalisation level of learning

With internalisation, learning has been incorporated into the behaviour of the student, part of the life style influencing both actions and attitudes. Assessment at this level should attempt to reveal an ability to solve problems, analyse situations, interpret findings and express concepts. Surveys or small research studies, presentation of care studies and case histories are all activities that will enable the student to demonstrate such characteristics of learning and can also measure the achievement of objectives.

Assessment at the dissemination level of learning

Dissemination, the highest level of learning, involves the outward expression of learning. The student is now the 'teacher'; she has the desire to stimulate and inform others, even to impress her learning upon others. Because the bulk of this behaviour is overt, it is assessable. The supervisor will not only be looking for abilities to solve problems, analyse and interpret situations and data but also the degree of influence the student has on others. What are her values and how well developed are her judgemental skills? Does she have the ability to act as advocate and counsellor? Assessment will involve submission of critical analyses of care plans and evaluations by the student to her supervisor. The student will readily demonstrate an ability to teach and behave as a role model to others. Student self-assessment, peer assessment and the desire to set objectives for continuing development all confirm that the dissemination level has been achieved.

Conclusion

As the student progresses through the levels of learning from exposure to an experience to its ultimate dissemination, so the supervisor passes from being an observer, questioner and measurer to an appraiser of the student with the task of judging to what extent the learning experiences in the clinical setting have influenced the student's behaviour.

References

Bevis E O (1978) *Curriculum Building in Nursing*. St Louis: Mosby
Chater S (1979) In Bower F L & Bevis E O (eds) *Fundamentals of Nursing Practice; Concepts, Roles and Functions*. St Louis: Mosby
Childs D (1985) *Psychology and the Teacher*. New York: Holt, Rinehart & Winston
Curzon L B (1985) *Teaching in Further Education*. New York: Holt, Rinehart & Winston
Department of Health & Social Security (1983) *The Nurses, Midwives and Health Visitors Rules Approval Order 1983* (Cmd 873). London: H M S O
Halsbury Lord (1974) *Report of the Committee of Enquiry into Pay and Related Conditions of Nurses and Midwives*. London: H M S O
Kelly A V (1982) *The Curriculum, Theory and Practice*. London: Harper & Row
Roper N et al (1983) *Using a Model for Nursing*. Edinburgh: Churchill Livingstone

Taylor S G (1985) In Riehl-Sisca J (ed) *The Science and Art of Self-care*. Norwalk, Connecticut: Appleton Century Crofts

Tyler R W (1949) *Basic Principles of Curriculum and Instruction*. University of Chicago Press

United Kingdom Central Council (1986) Project 2000: *A New Preparation for Practice*. London: U K C C

4
The Principles of Assessment

There is no more contentious subject in education and training than that of assessment and examinations. Minton (1984) asserts that: 'Teachers and society are content with relatively unsophisticated achievement tests which often do not differentiate between the many things that they may be measuring together.' More cynically, it has been suggested that examinations measure the ability to pass examinations! Indeed, it has to be acknowledged that for many students examinations are a bizarre but deadly serious game, the rules and conduct of which may have only limited relevance to the course of study they are undertaking or, in the case of a final qualifying examination, the job that examination success will license them to do. Nurse education does not and should not seek exemption from such criticism; indeed the profession has expressed disquiet concerning the validity of its examinations for many years. More recently, the rate of failure in nursing examinations has become an issue of public concern. For the purpose of awarding qualification, nursing has tended to employ a narrow band of crude achievement tests biased towards simple skills and the less complex cognitive abilities. Much of the criticism of nursing assessment procedures is justified. However, such criticism rarely argues against the need for examinations, but is levelled at examinations of poor quality which fail to fulfil their proper function, or aim to fulfil functions for which they are inappropriate.

With individual schools of nursing now assuming greater responsibility for examination procedures and the shifting emphasis towards continuous assessment, there is an even greater requirement for nursing and nurse education to examine its examinations. Additionally, the changing role of the nurse demands a new generation of skills and competences that will require appropriate assessment strategies. In this respect assessment methods that have only achieved limited success in the past are destined to failure in the future.

Defining assessment

Assessment suffers from being well known and, in some respects, little understood. This is reflected in the numerous and conflicting definitions of assessment

43

and the number of terms that are used synonymously with it. Already in this chapter 'examinations' and 'tests' have been used in this way. For some, assessment is an omnibus term that includes all the process and products that describe the nature and extent of learning, and additionally includes measures of the social and economic value of the curriculum. For the purposes of this discussion assessment is defined as:

> 'Measurement that directly relates to the quality and quantity of learning and as such is concerned with student progress and attainment'.

This deliberately restrictive definition assumes assessment to be distinct from, but subordinate to, evaluation. Evaluation is concerned with measuring the overall worth of the curriculum itself and not exclusively the effectiveness of its procedures and will be considered separately and in detail in Chapter 9.

The argument against assessment

It might seem to be common sense that students undertaking a course of training should be assessed, but to assume unthinkingly that students should be examined denies a complex debate concerning the purpose of examinations and, indeed, the need for examinations at all. Satterly (1981) has undertaken a comprehensive study of the issues involved and although the debate focuses, in particular, on primary and secondary education, it is worth remembering that our students are products of this system, as we are, and that frequently nurse education has, at least in the past, looked to general education for guidance and has assimilated some of its values and procedures. Objections often raised against examinations are:

1   *Assessment is a political activity that preserves the social order of society.* Consequently, examinations perpetuate the existing hierarchical structure of society, resulting in the application of labels which determine the individual's opportunities in life. This argument can certainly be applied to student nurse selection. Whatever additional criteria are used to select student nurses, the statutory educational requirements are 'a minimum of five subjects at Ordinary level A, B or C grade in the General Certificate of Education' (Rule 16(1) a) (D H S S 1983). There can be no doubt that 'good' intelligence is required to complete nurse training successfully and five O-level passes require such intelligence. However, such success also demands appropriate social circumstances such as a stable and supportive home environment and a secondary school that is able to afford appropriate teaching and learning opportunities. These variables are, of course, independent of intelligence. However, schools of nursing have demonstrated a reticence to employ direct measures of intelligence as permitted by Rule 16(1)e: 'a specified standard in an educational test approved by the Council', and as such could be accused of maintaining the social order! It is also possible that many enrolled nurses will identify with an argument that suggests that examinations label, categorise and restrict opportunities. Nursing would find it difficult to deny the

existence of a system of 'professional apartheid' that actively denies enrolled nurses personal and professional development.

2 *Assessment is limited to relatively trivial educational objectives whilst the most important aims of schooling are inaccessible to testing.* The problems associated with identifying and stating educational objectives were discussed in the previous chapter. These clearly have implications for the nature and quality of assessments that are used to determine whether the objectives have been achieved. There can be no doubt that 'set-piece' ward-based clinical assessments in an attempt to measure student performance objectively may have a tendency to focus on relatively trivial aspects of nursing performance. This criticism can also be levelled at a variety of other assessments. Satisfactory objective test items are notoriously difficult to construct and many tests, particularly of the multiple-choice type, require merely recall or recognition of facts for successful completion.

3 *The results of assessment have an uncanny knack of being self-fulfilling.* Expectations can be influenced by assessment in two distinct ways: the teacher's expectancy of students and the students' expectancy of their own future performance. In the latter case the results of assessment are incorporated into the individuals' concept of themselves. Early in a course of training, dependent on the results of assessments, students develop a success or failure identity. Consequently, they may, with limited justification, believe themselves to be 'good' or 'bad' at a particular subject or skill. The student who succeeds expects future success. 'Nothing breeds success — like success', and is motivated accordingly. In contrast, the student who fails may withdraw from further attempts to learn. Those responsible for teaching and assessing develop expectations of their student nurses' performance; these are partially based on 'formal assessments' but also on influences such as the student's appearance, social background and speech. These expectations are then reflected in the type of clinical work a student is allocated, the difficulty of a question asked in the classroom or the level of concern and interest a teacher demonstrates to a particular student. These expectations are, consciously or otherwise, transmitted to the student and, consequently, students perform in the way we expect them to perform. Of the 'self-fulfilling prophecy' Satterly observes: 'The overall result of a teacher's assessment can be detrimental for those students who are set low expectations and correspondingly damaging for those, who because of an unreliably optimistic assessment, are set levels they are quite unable to fulfil.'

4 *Assessment encourages the student to develop the styles of thought and intellectual 'tricks' required by tests and therefore inhibits the development of other skills.* Miller & Partlett (1974) suggest that students perceive examinations to be a game which is irrelevant to real life and, consequently, they study the rules of the game so as to be good at it. These students who do consistently better in examinations than their peers, Miller & Partlett call 'cue-seekers'. They scrutinise previous examination papers, discover their teachers' main interests and actively attempt to detect hints of likely examination questions in the words of their teachers. Subsequently, they invest their energy in rehearsing probable examination questions. Of course, such

activity is quite legitimate but in concentrating their studies they are also diluting their level of achievement. Rowley (1974) has demonstrated that tactics can contribute significantly to results of multiple-choice tests. Students who are prepared to take risks score higher than students with equivalent knowledge and ability who do not.

5   *Assessment inevitably takes place in a role relationship. This is antithetical to a truly educational setting where encounters between teachers and students are interpersonal.* As assessment is made by someone about someone, this produces a hierarchical and authoritarian relationship between the teacher and the student. This preoccupation with teacher-dominated assessment Knowles (1973) describes as being 'progressively recessive', denying students responsibility for learning and inhibiting self-criticism, self-assessment, self-reliance, independence and creativity. The judgemental and authoritarian 'I — It' relationship between teacher and student is a feature of pedagogy (the art and science of teaching children). However, it appears to be the model that is frequently applied to adult education, including nurse education. In contrast, andragogy (the art and science of teaching adults) advocates an equal and non-judgemental relationship between teacher and student, a relationship of mutual trust and respect that can be summarised as 'I–Thou'. This inevitably has implications for the role and nature of assessments.

The arguments against examinations are powerful and have probably gained momentum in recent years because, in many instances, education has denied their existence or chosen to ignore them. However, as suggested earlier in this chapter the criticism of assessment is essentially a criticism of abuse. Appropriately designed schemes of assessment are an integral part of the curriculum rather than a 'bolt-on bit' that dominates and intimidates the curriculum process. Assessments that are designed with an acknowledgement of their limitations and seek to maximise their merits and minimise their demerits are vital, indeed essential, to nurse training.

The purpose of assessment

Having acknowledged the arguments against assessment, the reader may question why do we assess? There are many and various reasons for assessment: Klug (1971), according to Bligh (1975), has identified 32 purposes of assessment. In contrast, the English National Board (1986) suggests there are just two fundamental reasons for assessing student nurses. For purposes of this discussion the classification proposed by Bligh (1975) will be used.

To licence nurses as competent practitioners

Donald Bligh considers this the least important reason for assessment and examinations. He argues, with justification, that professional qualifying examinations may license individuals to do things that were not a feature of their course of training. Certainly, a 'basic' nurse training course does not confer all the clinical skills that a newly qualified staff nurse may be required to possess. However, the public have a fundamental entitlement to expect competence from the trained nurse and indeed to be protected against incompetence. The machinery of Statutory Registration is designed to ensure that those legally entitled to call themselves nurses possess the competencies identified in Rules 18(1) and 18(2) and are safe practitioners. However, Bligh's reservations cannot be ignored, and are not. They are addressed by the U K C C Code of Professional Conduct 1984 (2nd ed):

> 'Each registered nurse, midwife and health visitor is accountable for his or her practice and in exercise of professional accountability shall:
> 4   Acknowledge any limitations of competence and refuse in such cases to accept delegated functions without first having received instruction in regard to those functions and having been assessed as competent.'

However, qualifying and licensing procedures such as nurse registration share some of the characteristics of the Driving Test or the M O T Certificate awarded to a motor vehicle — i.e. requirements of the test, or nursing competence, was demonstrated at the time of registration. Obviously, skills can decay or essential new skills not be developed. The U K C C demand that nurses retain their competence:

> 3   ' . . . shall:
> Take every reasonable opportunity to maintain and improve professional knowledge and competence.'   .

However, providing nurses with the appropriate resources and opportunities for retaining and developing their skills has been, until relatively recently, an area of gross neglect. This issue will be more fully considered when the continuing education and training of nurses is discussed in Chapter 6.

To predict the future behaviour of nurses

Assessments should measure what they purport to measure; in other words, they should be valid. The validity of an assessment has a number of dimensions. Examinations should look right! For example, an assessment of the student's ability to receive and admit a patient into hospital using a written test may reveal that they understand the principles but will not confirm they possess the complex array of observational, analytical, interpersonal and technical skills required. A written test in this example would lack *face validity*. Additionally, an assessment should have *concurrent validity*; this means that if two different assessments are designed to measure the achievement of the same objective then the student should do equally well (or otherwise) on both — there should be a positive correlation between both assessments. There is a degree of circularity here because if we have constructed an assessment that correlates highly with another, what is the point of the new one? *Predictive validity* is the most severe test of a test, the most difficult to achieve, yet probably one of the most important purposes of assessment. When student nurses are admitted to training they have satisfied the assessment procedures of the school of nursing that they have the potential to complete successfully a course of nurse training — a prediction has been made. In view of the unacceptably high rate of attrition of students during training, the predictive validity of the selection techniques employed is highly questionable. Possibly the most significant development and contribution to our understanding of the selection of students is that made by the Student Nurse Selection Project at the University of Leeds. The research findings and proposals of this D H S S-funded project should provide those responsible for the selection of student nurses with clearer principles upon which to base their decision-making and therefore substantially improve the predictive validity of student nurse selection.

Throughout nurse training, *formative* (continuing) assessments are being made which in themselves are predictive. Permitting a student to proceed to the next module of training and clinical experience is in itself implicit, if not explicit, evidence that they are ready to proceed and there is an expectation or prediction that they will be successful. However, the contemporary reality is that only the most severe educational doubts could prevent a student from proceeding to the next experience because of the dependency of nursing service provision on student nurses. Additionally, the employee status of student nurses means that educational failure has disciplinary consequences, ultimately that of dismissal. Poor educational management and indifferent labour relations may well conspire to permit a student who is patently unsuitable to proceed with training; however, for as long as a student remains in training it must be assumed that success is being predicted. Of course, the injustices of this iniquitous situation will be resolved when 'nurses' in training are completely independent of manpower provision and their status is that of student and not of employee of the National Health Service.

Finally, an overall assessment has to be made that will permit the student to register as a nurse. Yet another prediction is being made — that for as long as they remain a Registered Practitioner they will be competent. This clearly is the most difficult of predictions; the changing role of the nurse and adoption of new and diverse competencies will demand an equally diverse approach to assessment. Since the publication of Bendall's (1975) thesis, it has been acknowledged that what students say they do at assessment and what they actually do in clinical practice is not necessarily the same thing. It is evident that many schemes of assessment have cognisance of this. However, Bendall's findings are salutory to those wishing to predict the future behaviour of nurses.

To judge the level of student achievement

Throughout the course of training it is essential that students should be aware of their level of achievement. Examinations that measure a broad range of achievement at the conclusion of a course, e.g. a final examination, are described as *summative*. In contrast, *formative* assessments are the more discrete assessments that take place throughout the duration of a course to determine that a particular skill or series of skills have been accomplished, or to test acquisition of and ability to use particular theoretical concepts. The purpose of such assessments is to measure the student's development and progress. Achievement tests have different characteristics:

Norm-referenced assessment   This is a test of the individual's achievement in comparison with others who have taken the same examination or assessment; subsequently, students can be placed in rank order of achievement 'first to last', 'best to worst'. Such an approach is used when the demand for a particular education or professional opportunity exceeds the places available. Consequently, the 'best' 60 per cent, or whatever, can be selected. The 11-plus examination that gives access to grammar school education (in a few parts of the country) is of this type, as indeed are nurse selection tests in many instances. It is also apparent that many professional and academic examinations have these characteristics to judge by the almost 'fixed' percentage that pass and fail the examination on each occasion. As examinations of this type are inevitably somewhat 'secretive' it is difficult to say with certainly if this is really the case. If it is not, the persistent and frequently relatively high failure rate brings into question the validity of student selection, the appropriateness of the course design and the quality of teaching. The 'injustices' of such an approach are self-evident — the examination is essentially competitive and the 'ability' of those competing can vary considerably from examination to examination. Consequently, a student presenting precisely the same examination script could pass on one occasion and fail on another. In determining failure or success, norm-referenced assessment has no place in nurse education.

Criterion-referenced assessment   In contrast to norm-referenced assessment, criterion-referenced assessments measure the student's skills and abilities against quite specific and predetermined criteria. The issue here for the assessor is quite clear: whether the student has demonstrated the competencies required (criteria) of this particular assessment. Such criteria which relate directly to the objectives of the course are frequently 'formally' expressed. When assessing clinical skills, a checklist or rating scale may be employed; with written assessments a marking plan specifying the criteria will be used. This, of course, grossly oversimplifies the situation because as the complexity of the skill being assessed increases, so does the difficulty in expressing criteria, and consequently objective decisions in assessment are increasingly displaced by subjective judgements.

Other achievement tests   In addition to norm-referenced and criterion-referenced assessments, tests of achievement can be classified as *mastery tests* or *survey tests*. With mastery tests a clear PASS or FAIL decision is made. Such an approach can be used for measuring clinical competence when the assessor simply wishes to determine whether the student is competent or not. Of course, such an approach conceals the comparative 'excellence' of students; however, it does mean that an 'above average' performance in one component of an assessment does not eclipse inadequacy or incompetence in another part of the same assessment, and vice versa.

Alternatively, a survey test assumes a 'normal distribution' of abilities and marks or grades are awarded to reflect individual student levels of achievement.

Clearly, such differences in student performance and ability are real enough. Comparing a student's succession of grades/marks enables the assessor and student to quantify progress in a more meaningful way than simple PASS/FAIL data permits. However, it has to be acknowledged that awarding precise marks, e.g. as a percentage, is notoriously difficult. Unless the basis for the award of marks is very precise and based on specific, measurable criteria, the powers of discrimination required may elude any assessor. Consequently, the same piece of assessed work might receive considerably different marks from different examiners. In this situation the grade or mark awarded may more accurately reflect the ability of the examiner than that of the student.

To monitor student progress

It is necessary that students and their teachers should be able to monitor the level of achievement as the course progresses. As previously described in Chapter 2, a knowledge of results, reinforcement and reward are important learning principles. A sequence of intermittent assessments enables the students' progress to be monitored. In isolation, the assessment will reveal the students' location relative to their own personal learning objectives and objectives of the specific unit of the course, but it also provides information on their performance relative to these previous assessments and relative to the performance of other students. Monitoring individual and group performance enables the early detection of students' learning difficulties and the implementation of appropriate remedial action.

In recent years it has been unfashionable, indeed often offensive, to legitimise the role of competition in education. There is no doubt that creating a ruthless climate of competition is damaging for all concerned. After all, assessment in nurse education should not be competitive (norm-referenced) and the prize of registration is accessible to all who have commenced training, theoretically at least. However, it has also to be acknowledged that much of man's ingenuity, creativity, inventiveness and productivity can be directly traced to competitiveness. Whether students should be encouraged to compare their assessment results is clearly a contentious issue. The reality is that with or without our consent our students compare their grades and marks, success and failure. It might be that promoting a climate of gentle competitiveness in assessment would be more healthy and honest than the fraudulent denial of the existence of competition.

To motivate students

It is self-evident that most students become increasingly conscientious about their studies as the time of an assessment approaches. In the main this is healthy and desirable, although motivation for achievement and the perceived need to study should be a by-product of assessment and not one of its major purposes. The nature of a course of nurse training should have sufficient intrinsic worth to the individual that 'fear of failure' should not be an overwhelming influence. However, the amount of time devoted to study does increase as examinations approach, as does the individual's level of arousal and anxiety. Still (1963) has demonstrated that the incidence of psychiatric referrals among university students increases as examinations approach. It could be assumed that assessment-related stress is, in the main, a problem associated with courses that have a 'one-off' final examination, as indeed it is, and that this will be diminished with schemes of continuous assessment. However, it can be argued that with continuous assessment that level of stress is merely more evenly distributed throughout the entire course. In Chapter 2 the relationship between arousal and performance was illustrated; the issue of stress will be more fully discussed in Chapter 6.

To measure the effectiveness of teaching

It is not unreasonable to assume that the achievement of students, as measured by examination success, is in part related to the effectiveness of their teachers. Indeed, teachers appear readily to associate themselves with their students' success. Paradoxically, student failure is more likely to be perceived as being the fault of the students rather than that of the teacher. Further, there is a tendency for teachers to assert that it is unfair to measure their performance merely on the outcome of their students' assessments. At a time when increasingly quality assurance and value for money are a concern for all public services including the health service, there is need to identify indicators of performance. Although other indices of the effectiveness of teaching are being developed, the achievement of students will continue to be used as a measure of the effectiveness of teaching. In this context assessment is an issue of accountability and evaluation, and will be further discussed in Chapter 9.

Assessment strategy

The past twenty-five years has witnessed not so much a change in assessment techniques as a change in assessment strategy. Clearly, there have been innovations in assessment methods but in the main it is the focus of assessments and their relationship to the course overall that has altered. In this respect a number of dimensional changes can be identified; these are illustrated in Fig. 4.1.

Many other dimensions could be considered but these ones are illustrated as being representative. However, it should be noted that the respective progress on each dimension has not been uniform and whilst a radical shift has occurred on some axes, the shift is barely discernible on others.

The detailed identification and analysis of educational objectives into cognitive, affective and psychomotor categories undertaken by Benjamin Bloom and his associates was discussed in Chapter 2. Scrutiny of nursing curricula reveals that this tripartite structuring of human abilities is much favoured by nurse educationists. Course objectives are frequently presented under the distinct headlines of (1) knowledge, (2) attitudes and (3) skills. However, when it comes to assessment, methods of determining achievement in the cognitive (knowledge) domain appear to have been far more extensively developed than those in the affective (attitudes) or psychomotor (skills) categories. Assessment grids and marking schemes that employ a cognitive taxonomy are relatively common, but

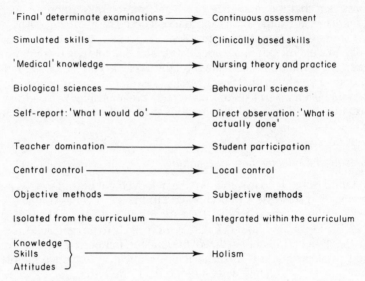

Fig. 4.1   Dimensional changes in assessment

those relating to the affective and psychomotor domain have been conspicuous by their absence. Inevitably this means that there is a potential for cognition or theory to dominate assessment, as it most certainly has. One possible explanation is that in the wake of general education and encouraged by the statutory

Table 4.1   Experiential taxonomy – assessment methods (Steinaker & Bell 1979)

Exposure	Observing student reaction to the initial activities to determine attention; understanding of terms, scenes and purpose; and readiness and/or willingness to proceed
Participation	Examining student choices; signals of understanding or of lack of understanding; replications; discussions; questioning to determine understanding; ability to succeed; and, where appropriate, explanation of how the learner 'would do it' if given the opportunity
Identification	Using criteria, teacher-developed tests or assignments, and mental or actual checklists to assess student progress and teaching or unit effectiveness
Internalisation	Using projective measures such as open-ended anonymous response questionnaires and/or direct measures such as rating scales and interviews; using a post- and retest method in which a different test form or assignment is given at a later date and is compared with the original test or assignment to determine retention
Dissemination	Using student self-assessment instruments; assessing the time devoted to tasks, the variety of techniques employed to use or to promote the learning and/or the degree of influence achieved

bodies, nurse education has jumped on a cognitive–behavioural bandwagon in an attempt to appear 'objective' and 'scientific' in pursuit of 'legitimising' itself as a learned discipline (Forgan-Morle 1984).

Alternatively or additionally, an 'experiential' approach, because of its holistic view of abilities, does not permit any domain to be neglected during assessment. Steinaker & Bell (1979) identify specific assessment techniques that they recommend should be employed at each level of their taxonomy in Table 4.1.

In addition to this 'whole student' perspective of assessment, such an approach ensures that the assessment techniques are compatible with the abilities being measured. Further, and significantly, assessment is congruent with the other components of curricular activity and in this respect domination of the curriculum by assessment is averted. It should also be noted that student self-asessment is an explicit requirement of the taxonomy; this is characteristic of the andragogical approach discussed earlier in this chapter. In relation to the 'teacher-domination–student-participation' dimension there is considerable evidence that techniques and instruments of self-assessment are being developed — but by whom? Students should also assume the responsibility of contributing to the design of the assessment tools that are to be employed.

References

Bendall E (1975) *So You Passed, Nurse!* London: R C N

Bligh D (1975) *Teaching Students.* Exeter: U E T S

Department of Health & Social Security (1983) *Nurses, Midwives and Health Visitors Rules Approval Order 1983* (Cmd 873). London: H M S O

English National Board (1986) *Guidelines to Preparing Continuous Assessment* (86/16). London: E N B

Forgan-Morle K M (1984) The problems in evaluating student nurses. *Nurse Education Today,* **4**(4)

Klug E C (1971) *Student Profiles.* Cambridge: Lutterworth Press

Knowles M (1973) *The Adult Learner A Neglected Species.* Houston: Gulf Publishing

Miller C & Parlett M (1974) *Up to the Mark: A Study of the Examination Game.* London: Society for Research into Higher Education

Minton D (1984) Evaluation and assessment in continuing education. In *Teaching Strategies for Continuing Education.* London: City & Guilds Institute

Rowley G L (1974) Which examinees are most favoured by the use of multiple choice tests? *Journal of Educational Measurement,* **11**, 15–23

Satterly D (1981) *Assessment in Schools.* Oxford: Basil Blackwell

Steinaker N & Bell R (1979) *The Experiential Taxonomy: A New Approach to Teaching and Learning.* New York: Academic Press

Still R J (1963) *Psychological Illness among Students in the Examination Period.* University of Leeds

United Kingdom Central Council (1984) *Code of Professional Conduct,* 2nd ed. London: U K C C

5
Methods of Assessment

In the previous chapter the necessity for compatibility and congruity of assessment techniques was identified. Before considering the various methods at our disposal, it is worth looking at the increasingly important issue of continuous assessment. From the point of view of classification it may well have been more correct to discuss continuous assessment under the heading of the previous section, for it is essentially a strategy of assessment rather than a method.

Continuous assessment

The English National Board (1986) has issued guidelines on preparing schemes of continuous assessment (86/16) and clearly it would be redundant to simply reiterate their advice. However, it is worth while to identify briefly the main principles and issues concerned. Continuous assessment has been variously defined and can be described as: ' . . . a planned series of progressively updated measurements of student achievement and progress, that are concerned with "whom" and by "whom", rather than "how" ' (E N B 1986). The impetus for continuous assessment can be directly attributed to the patent injustice of 'one-off' final and determinate examinations where the competence demonstrated 'on the day' may not be representative of the abilities demonstrated by the student throughout the course, where factors such as luck or anxiety may unfairly influence her performance. In practice, the use of a broader range of assessment techniques, more frequent assessment of student progress and achievement and the involvement of more individual assessors all conspire to dilute the deficiencies of traditional 'one-off' examinations. However, continuous assessment brings with it its own problems. Poorly conceived schemes have the potential to subject the students to multiple rather than the former occasional abuse. The potential to replace the 'acute' anxiety of a final examination by a course-long 'chronic' variant must also be acknowledged. A further and possibly more insidious problem is concerned with the implications for the teacher–student relationship. It is suggested that continuous assessment may create an authoritarian and strained relationship that is not conducive to a free flow of ideas. Athough teachers have always assessed their students, the ultimate responsibility for giving a student access to professional licence and registration now resides locally rather than with some external and anonymous examiner. This has subtle and potentially damaging implications for a relationship that should be based on mutual trust. From an administrative perspective, continuous assessment, by virtue of the increased number of measurements, can pose difficulties. Poor planning and poor management may cause spasms where teachers and students are overloaded by the requirements of course work assessment. However, as long as the limitations and potential problems of continuous assessment are addressed, the strategy is a more equitable approach to assessing nursing competence than the former system of examinations.

Objective and subjective methods

Beattie & Bessent (1986) identify two intersecting dimensions of assessment and have plotted the location of a variety of assessment methods relative to each of these dimensions in Fig. 5.1.

This is a particularly illuminating illustration of the methods of assessment employed in nurse education which it is worth while studying to identify the methods that are most commonly used. The evidence that is available would seem to suggest that 'objective' methods of assessment dominate the curriculum, although not entirely to the exclusion of more 'subjective' techniques. However,

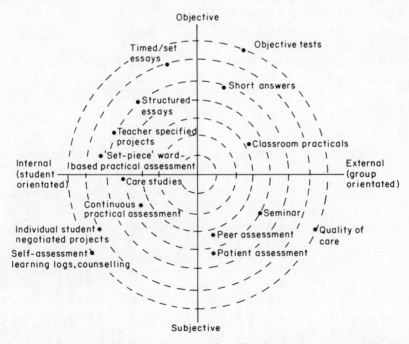

Fig. 5.1   Dimensions and orientation in modes of student assessment (modified from Beattie & Bessent 1986)

Please score all items by entering a tick in the appropriate column. Failure to do so will reduce the effectiveness of this Assessment.

	PROGRESS VERY GOOD	PROGRESS GOOD	PROGRESS JUST GOOD ENOUGH	PROGRESS UNSATIS-FACTORY	
A. TO WORK					
1. Industrious and keen					Apathetic and slow
2. Shows initiative in all situations					Finds great difficulty in adapting
3. Appears to be prompt and conscientious in the performance of her duties					Does not appear to be prompt and conscientious in the performance of her duties
4. Always neat, well groomed and appropriately dressed					Not always neat, well groomed and appropriately dressed
5. Achieves and maintains a high quality of performance in all aspects of work					Overall quality of performance is consistently poor
COMMENTS					

	PROGRESS VERY GOOD	PROGRESS GOOD	PROGRESS JUST GOOD ENOUGH	PROGRESS UNSATIS-FACTORY	
B. TO PATIENTS					
1. Successfully anticipates and meets the needs of patients					Sometimes fails to recognise and meet the needs of patients
2. Shows exceptional understanding of patients as individual persons					Seldom manages to adapt her/his approach to suit needs of individuals
3. Shows outstanding skill in gaining confidence and co-operation of patients; tactful and considerate					As yet unskilled in gaining confidence and co-operation of patients
4. Shows better ability than most in dealing tactfully and courteously with patients, relatives and visitors					Sometimes omits to show courtesy and understanding in dealing with patients, relatives and visitors
COMMENTS					

C. TO COWORKERS

1. Reliable, works well as a member of the ward team				Appears to have difficulty working as a member of the ward team
2. Distinguished by courtesy and helpfulness towards other members of hospital staff				Sometimes appears rather off-hand in dealings with other members of hospital staff
3. Responds with good grace to instructions/advice. Makes the most of constructive criticism				Often appears reluctant to accept instruction and constructive criticism
				TOTAL

COMMENTS

Fig. 5.2 Specimen of a nursing progress report

an audit of assessment methods in many schools of nursing would weigh heavily in favour of the upper quadrants of Fig. 5.1. This would be a satisfactory, indeed entirely appropriate situation, if nursing were a 'pure' and precise science and the skills of nursing lent themselves to 'scientific' and objective measurement. However, the model(s) of nursing that the profession subscribes to, although including 'scientific' components, also portrays nursing as a 'humanistic' and subjective art; consequently, the perpetual search for objective criteria and the elimination of subjective judgement is not possible, or even desirable. It could be argued that confining our endeavours to objective assessment at the expense of subjective judgement means that significant individual student learning achievements are being obscured, if not concealed. The adoption of a balanced scheme of assessment that employs assessment methods from all four orientations of Fig. 5.1 would provide more global, comprehensive and accurate assessment of student nurse competence.

Assessing clinical nursing competence

The relative advantages and disadvantages of a range of assessment methods are considered in the final section of this chapter. The objective of this section is to discuss what assessent methods and strategies can be employed clinically to determine the student's competence. Historically, this was measured indirectly by a practical test in simulated conditions. More recently, a system of 'ward-based assessments' directly examined a restricted, albeit important, series of skills in the clinical environment in which the student was working. The limitations of these approaches, including artificiality, predictability and restrictiveness are self-evident. A further and major contribution to clinical assessment has been the use of the King's Fund (1972) nurses' progress report and its many modifications that are in current use (Fig. 5.2).

However, despite modifications to reflect the different philosophies and needs of individual schools of nursing, there are fundamental problems with this type of instrument. Firstly, there is a tendency towards 'generalising' skills, so that significant but discrete levels of achievement are concealed. Further, each of the dimensions are weighted equally, although in reality some skills may be more significant or important than others. In the example given (Fig. 5.2), a student who is industrious, prompt, well-groomed and courteous could be graded overall as 'progress very good' despite being 'just good enough' on all other dimensions. Would this be a valid measure of the progress being made by the student in achieving nursing competence? Finally, when the same instrument is used throughout training it has similar properties to elastic in the sense that, despite radical changes in student behaviour through the acquisition of numerous skills, it stretches around an increasing number of accomplishments enabling the units of measurement to remain the same. In this respect 'progress' is a misnomer — when you have to keep running to stay in precisely the same place it is difficult to measure what has been achieved!

Despite the criticism of these methods, in 'isolation' each of these techniques has its own considerable merits, but as a collective strategy of clinical assessment could be criticised for being insufficiently coherent and comprehensive. Con-

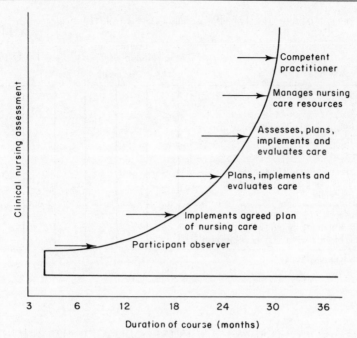

Fig. 5.3   Assessment of clinical nursing skills

temporary strategies of clinical assessment demand the continuous assessment of students that demonstrates the acquisition of an increasingly sophisticated range of skills as the course progresses. Fig. 5.3 demonstrates this.

Methods of clinical assessment

In assessing the complex array of skills illustrated in Fig. 5.3, a variety of techniques are required. At best, individual assessments are a bit like taking 'snapshots' — the picture reveals precisely what was happening at the instant the film was exposed. Consequently, the more 'snaps' that are taken from various angles, the greater our overall impression and understanding of what is being looked at. There is also a case for passing the 'camera' around as different individuals may wish to focus on alternative aspects of the subject, including the student taking self-portraits. To develop this analogy further it may well be that some of our shots will be out of focus, but as long as that is recognised, important though restricted information will still be available. What is being advocated here is the need for comprehensive portrayal of student abilities. Such an approach is described as *profiling*. Law (1984) describes a whole range of methods of student portrayal which have been developed ' . . . to replace — or at least supplement — conventional assessment formats'. The techniques described here represent some nursing applications.

3. CREATES A THERAPEUTIC LEARNING ENVIRONMENT FOR THE CHILD

	Learner Self-appraisal			Final Gradings		
	H C	C	IC	H C	C	IC
3.1 Involves the child in aspects of daily living						
3.2 Provides a stimulating environment which encourages suitable activities for the age group of the child						
3.3 Organises and participates in play situations using appropriate equipment and materials						
3.4 Recognises and applies a safe environment for the child whilst being aware of the effects of over protection (*)						

COMMENT (if necessary)

4. APPRECIATES THE IMPORTANCE OF INTERPERSONAL RELATIONSHIPS WITH THE CHILD

	Learner Self-appraisal			Final Gradings		
	H C	C	IC	H C	C	IC
4.1 Establishes rapport with the child (*)						
4.2 Communicates effectively verbally/non-verbally with the child						
4.3 Encourages social interaction amongst the children						
4.4 Creates a healthy and homely atmosphere for the benefit of the child						
4.5 Demonstrates empathy with the child's problems (*)						

COMMENT (if necessary)

Fig. 5.4   Assessment of practical competence

Supervisors/tutors assessments

Assessment of practical competence   This is an extract from an instrument that is designed for one specific clinical experience (nursing mentally handicapped children). It relates directly to the learning objectives of the experience, requires student self-assessment and permits negotiation of the final grading. Distinction is made between highly competent (HC), competent (C) and incompetent (IC) performance. The designers of this instrument have also identified what they consider to be critical (*) skills (Fig. 5.4).

General progress grid   This instrument is designed to measure a generalised range of abilities, and was originally devised for use in Hertfordshire secondary schools. Its purpose is not dissimilar to the King's Fund progress report. However, it has distinct advantages in that it is more specific about behaviours, its structure more readily permits pre- and postexperience measurement to be revealed on the same document and it more accurately indicates progress throughout the duration of a course. A nursing adaptation of this grid, for example, might require a student to attain a specified skills level I to IV at a particular stage of training (Fig. 5.5).

Quality of care assessment   The two previous examples are, in the main, concerned with observing what the student does; a further approach is to assess the consequences of their actions by measuring the quality of care delivered. An increasing number of such instruments are available; Fig. 5.6 is a specimen of 'Monitor' (Ball *et al* 1983). The advantage of this type of instrument is that it is based on the nursing process so that skills relating to assessment, planning, implementation and evaluation can be measured independently or collectively. This is particularly useful in relation to measuring the progression of skills illustrated in Fig. 5.6. A further advantage is that measurements are gathered from a variety of sources such as nursing records, care plans, the students, patients, as well as by direct observation. As the quality of care instrument becomes a common tool of clinical practice its importance as a method of student assessment will increase.

Patient–client assessment

As recipients of the care delivered by students, patients/clients are a legitimate source of assessment data, but gaining access to the assessments that patients are most certainly making is fraught with ethical and practical problems. However, there is potential in further developing instruments such as the U M I S T 'What the Patient Thinks' questionnaire (Fig. 5.7) as a group-orientated method of clinical assessment. Such instruments have a broader utility as an index of the 'clinical learning environment'. This will be discussed in Chapter 6.

Self-assessment

Students' assessment of their own performance would seem susceptible to

Level / Skills	I	Int	Final	II	Int	Final	III	Int	Final	IV	Int	Final
Problem recognition	Can describe simple problem in limited fashion			Can clearly state a problem with some analysis			Can clearly state problem and specify most aspects of it			Can precisely define problem and enumerate all aspects of it		
Investigation	Can find information with guidance			Can use standard sources of information			Can assemble information from a variety of sources			Shows initiative in seeking and utilizing information from a wide range of sources		
Problem solving	Can follow routine procedures with guidance			Can fault-find following standard procedures			Can select alternative solutions to given problems			Can independently derive and implement solution to a variety of problems		

Evaluation	Can assess own work with guidance	Can assess own performance on routine tasks independently	Can assess own performance and identify possible improvements	Can assess own work critically, relate problems to original brief, suggest future work
Reading and writing	Can understand simple texts and write brief notes and reports	Can follow and give straight-forward descriptions and explanations	Can use instruction manuals etc. and write clear accurate reports	Can abstract and interpret information from a variety of sources and communicate this effectively
Talking and listening	Can understand simple instructions and give messages	Can follow and give straight-forward oral instructions	Can follow and give more complex instructions and speak easily about own work	Adept in most verbal encounters; can explain work to strangers in groups or individually

Fig. 5.5   Progress grid (© Hertfordshire County Council)

DEPENDENCY CATEGORY III PATIENTS
INSTRUCTIONS: Please tick one answer per question.
Assessor name .... Ward name .... Study start date ....
or Assessor code .... or Ward code .... Stop date ....

Source of information

Patient's code or initials

Was patient unconscious when admitted? NO YES

Is patient unconscious now? NO YES

SECTION A   PLANNING NURSING CARE
1 Assessing Patient on Admission

Records

a) DOES THE NURSE INTERVIEW/OBSERVE THE PATIENT FOR ASSESSMENT OF PROBLEMS WITHIN 12 HOURS AFTER ADMISSION? Look at chart/records for evidence of assessment. Man ask patient "When you were admitted, did a nurse come to talk with you about your illness or any special problems?" "How long after you were admitted did the nurse talk to you?"

No
Yes
Not available/ Not applicable
1

SCORE

Pursue for time only if evidence that assessment was made. Answer 'yes' only if there is evidence of a comprehensive assessment and it was done within 12 hours of admission.

'Assessment' means that the nurse interviewed and observed the patient to identify his habits and problems.

'Comprehensive' refers to mention of psychological, sociological and physical needs of patient.

Records/ check or ask patient

b) IF THE PATIENT HAS PHYSICAL DISABILITIES (E.G. IMPAIRED HEARING, VISION, SPEECH ETC.) ARE THEY RECORDED WITHIN 24 HOURS OF ADMISSION?

No
Yes
Not applicable
2

If nothing recorded, check patient. If patient has physical disabilities, code as 'No'. If patient does not have physical disabilities code as 'Not applicable'.

SCORE

ADMISSION?

Refers to statement of presence or absence of allergies.

	3
	SCORE

Ask patient/ d) IF THE PATIENT DEPENDS ON PROSTHETIC DEVICES FOR ACTIVITIES OF DAILY LIVING IS THIS RECORDED WITHIN 24 HOURS OF ADMISSION?

Prosthetic devices incluce dentures, spectacles, contact lenses, hearing aids, orthopaedic shoes or braces, artificial limbs.

	No
	Yes
	Not applicable
	4
	SCORE

Records e) ARE THE PATIENT'S ELIMINATION PATTERNS RECORDED WITHIN 24 HOURS OF ADMISSION?

Applies to patterns prior to present hospital stay.

	No
	Yes
	5
	SCORE

Records f) IS BEHAVIOUR INDICATIVE OF MENTAL–EMOTIONAL STATE RECORDED ON ADMISSION?

Applies to behaviour assessment such as 'alert', 'talkative', 'anxious', 'depressed'.

	No
	Yes
	6
	SCORE

Records g) IS A STATEMENT WRITTEN WITHIN 24 HOURS OF ADMISSION ON THE CONDITIONS OF THE SKIN?

Refers to dryness, absence or presence of skin lesions, localised colour, warmth etc. DO NOT accept general description such as 'pale'.

	No
	Yes
	7
	SCORE

Fig. 5.6 Monitor (Ball et al, 1983)

NURSES

(a) **Help**

On every single occasion that I needed help in the bath or toilet, the nurses were there to help me.

Except in a few instances, the nurses assisted me in the bath or toilet whenever I needed them.

Sometimes the nurses were not around when I needed help in the bath or toilet

I never needed help from the nurses when I was in the bath or toilet.

(b) *Response*

(i) Did you ever need to ring the bell for attention from the nurses?

YES

NO (Go to question 2biii)

There was no bell
(Go to question 2biii)

(ii) The speed at which the nurses attended to me when I rang the bell:

	Day	Night
Could not have been quicker	☐	☐
Was very fast, everything considered during the:	☐	☐
Was barely fast enough	☐	☐
(Tick for the day and the night)		

(iii) I had the impression that the nurses would usually only help me if I asked them to

STRONGLY AGREE

AGREE

DISAGREE

STRONGLY DISAGREE

(c) **Work**

(i) At no time did the nurses appear to find it difficult to cope with the work in the ward.

Apart from one or two occasions the nurses seemed to manage quite easily on the ward.

There were times when the nurses in my ward did not appear to be able to cope with the amount of work they had to do.

(ii) Generally speaking, the nurses had a number of routine duties to do, and we had to fit in around their tasks.

STRONGLY AGREE

AGREE

DISAGREE

STRONGLY DISAGREE

Fig. 5.7 'What the Patient Thinks' questionnaire (UMIST 1985)

(d) **Relationships**

(i) The nurses seemed to go out of their way to chat with us whenever they could.

☐

The nurses seemed to find time for a chat with us at some time during the day.

☐

The nurses seemed too busy to spend very much time with us, other than when they were actually doing something for us.

☐

For one reason or another the nurses spent little of their time on the ward talking to us.

☐

(ii) Some of the nurses made particular favourites of one or two of the patients which at times causes a feeling or resentment from some of the other patients

AGREE

☐

DISAGREE

☐

(e) **Insight**

Too few of the nurses seemed to realise what it was like for a person in my condition.

☐

I felt that most of the nurses had some idea of what my condition was like.

☐

With only one or two exceptions, the nurses seemed to know what it was like to be in my condition.

☐

(f) **Overall care**

(i) The care from the nurses was kind, gentle and sympathetic at all times.

☐

On the whole the nurses' care was more than adequate.

☐

I would say that the nurses gave me reasonable care during my stay

☐

There was, I feel, room for improvement in the nurses' care.

☐

(ii) Without exception, all the nurses gave an impression of dedication to looking after ill people and not just doing it because it was a job to be done.

☐

Most of the nurses seemed to be dedicated to nursing ill people and not just treating it as a routine job.

☐

Many nurses appeared to lack a real interest in nursing, beyond a job that needed doing.

☐

Remarkably few nurses gave an appearance of dedication to nursing theill, over and beyond doing a routine job.

☐

Fig. 5.7 (*contd.*)

abuse. American research appears to indicate that student self-ratings are usually a little generous; however, Bligh (1975) reports positive correlations between student self-ratings and those of their teachers, and concludes: 'If student's assessments of their own work are taken seriously, they, too, take it seriously'. As self-criticism and self-assessment are fundamental to professional competence, student self-ratings of clinical performance should not be perceived as optional

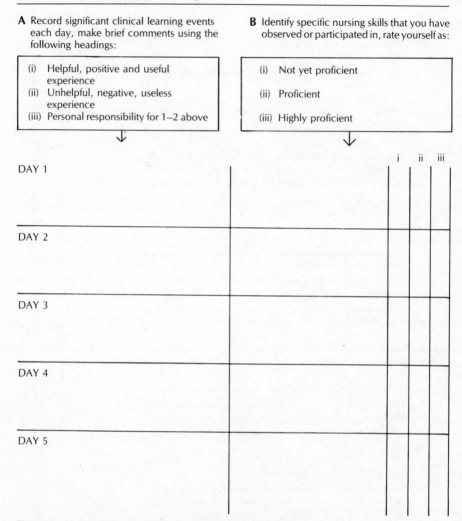

A Record significant clinical learning events each day, make brief comments using the following headings:

> (i)   Helpful, positive and useful experience
> (ii) Unhelpful, negative, useless experience
> (iii) Personal responsibility for 1–2 above

B Identify specific nursing skills that you have observed or participated in, rate yourself as:

> (i)   Not yet proficient
> (ii) Proficient
> (iii) Highly proficient

	i	ii	iii
DAY 1			
DAY 2			
DAY 3			
DAY 4			
DAY 5			

Fig. 5.8   Learning log — daily record of experience

but essential. Self-assessment can be incorporated into a number of the techniques previously described. *Counselling* is often considered as exclusively a technique for helping a student with a problem situation. However, client-centred problem-solving models of counselling demand goal-setting and problem-solving based on principles of self-assessment. In this context, counselling is a particularly useful method of self-assessment of clinical performance.

Role construct repertory tests and *grids* derived from Kelly's (1955) personal construct theory are powerful techniques for enabling students to reflect on their learning experiences. They have been used as a method of self-assessment in teacher training (Pope 1978). A nursing application of repertory grids is des-

	BEST NURSE	BETWEEN	AVERAGE NURSE	BETWEEN	POOREST NURSE	NOT APPLICABLE	NOT OBSERVED
Gives full attention to patient	( )	—	( )	—	( )	—	—
Is a receptive listener	( )	—	( )	—	( )	—	—
Approaches patient in a kind, gentle and friendly manner	( )	—	( )	—	( )	—	—
Responds in a therapeutic manner to patient's behaviour	( )	—	( )	—	( )	—	—
Recognises anxiety in patient and takes appropriate action	( )	—	( )	—	( )	—	—
Gives explanation and verbal reassurance when needed	( )	—	( )	—	( )	—	—
Offers companionship to patient without becoming involved in a non-therapeutic way	( )	—	( )	—	( )	—	—
Considers patient as a member of a family and of society	( )	—	( )	—	( )	—	—
Is alert to patient's spiritual needs	( )	—	( )	—	( )	—	—
Identifies individual needs expressed through behaviour and initiates actions to meet them	( )	—	( )	—	( )	—	—
Accepts rejection or ridicule and continues effort to meet needs	( )	—	( )	—	( )	—	—
Communicates belief in the worth and dignity of man	( )	—	( )	—	( )	—	—
Utilises healthy aspects of patient's personality	( )	—	( )	—	( )	—	—
Creates an atmosphere of mutual trust, acceptance, and respect, rather than showing concern for power, prestige and authority	( )	—	( )	—	( )	—	—
Conducts self with same professional demeanour when caring for an unconscious or disorientated patient as when caring for a conscious patient	( )	—	( )	—	( )	—	—

Fig. 5.9   Slater Nursing Competencies Rating Scale (an extract) (Wandelt & Slater 1975)

cribed by Nicklin (1984). Self-assessment is not synonymous with self-awareness but subordinate to it. The need to cultivate self-awareness in our students was considered in Chapter 2. Contemporary curricula give considerable prominence to the skills of self-awareness. The 1982 R M N Syllabus gives a detailed skills specification which include 'self-awareness is awareness of one's own: values, attitudes, prejudices, . . . , competence, skills and limitations; . . . body-language, . . . , attention to others, . . . genuineness, investment of self, effect on others, . . . , the intentional and conscious use of self.' How can these skills be assessed? McHale (1985) describes a variety of techniques, including psychometric tests, video feedback and personal and group analysis by an assessor trained in the technique of self-awareness assessment. *Learning Logs* and *records of experience* are a useful device for students to capture progressively information about their learning experiences. Subsequent reflection and analysis provide an opportunity for personal assessment of progress that can be compared with the impressions and opinions of supervisors, teachers and peers (Fig. 5.8).

Peer assessment

The student's peers have a significant contribution to make in the overall assessment process. Peer review and peer audit are increasingly features of professional nursing practice. As such, peer assessment during training provides the opportunities to develop the skills of receiving and giving appraisal and criticism of nursing competence. The fact that peers work for sustained periods in close proximity inevitably means they have the opportunity to make assessments that are inaccessible to others. Peer support groups and seminar groups provide the mechanism for peer assessment. Some of the instruments previously illustrated might include a peer assessment component. Fig. 5.9 is an extract from a nursing competencies rating scale developed by Slater (1975) and could be used for peer assessment.

The preparation and assessment of assessors

When the simulated 'practical tests' were replaced by 'ward-based assessments', the former General Nursing Council appointed experienced ward sisters and charge nurses to its panel of assessors. Initially, these appointments were based upon the recommendation of the individual's school of nursing and an interview conducted by officers of the Council. It is unlikely that such a selection process adequately assessed the individual's ability to assess. In recognition of this, the responsibility of appointing assessors was devolved directly to schools of nursing with a requirement to provide training in the 'art of assessment' for ward sisters. However, it has to be acknowledged that assessment is not the exclusive right or responsibility of ward sisters and teachers. There is a strong case for ensuring that all trained nurses are skilled in assessment and that such skills are developed within the initial or 'basic' registration course. Indeed, the statutory instruments are sufficiently explicit in this respect:

> Nurses, Midwives and Health Visitors Rules Approval Order 1983
> Rule 18(1) (f) ' . . . and where appropriate teach and co-ordinate other members of the caring team'.
> United Kingdom Council — Code of Professional Conduct 1984
> (12) ' . . . assist peers and subordinates to develop professional competence in accordance with their needs'.

What is implied here is that the assessment of students' clinical skills cannot be perceived as a 'take it or leave it' optional extra but is fundamental to the trained nurse's role — at the point of registration. However, as with all skills there is a need to retain and further develop competence: this is clearly an issue of continuing education and the concept will be fully explored in Chapter 6. With regard to assessment skills, a number of strategies can be employed.

Developing assessment skills

1   E N B 'postbasic' clinical studies courses provide an opportunity to review and develop assessment skills. All courses should include a 'teaching' objective: 'At the end of the course, the nurse will have increased understanding of the principles and methods of teaching and will be able to assess whether learners have achieved the objectives to the standard required' (J B C N S 1983).

More specifically, E N B Course 998 'Teaching and Assessing in Clinical Practice' is designed to enable clinical nurses to plan and provide a learning environment, to teach and use appropriate assessment procedures.

2   Further and higher education courses such as the Further Education Teachers Certificate (City and Guilds Institute) and Diploma in Nursing (University of London) provide opportunities to develop competence in assessment techniques.

3   In-service training courses such as 'The Art of Assessment' exclusively examine the skills of assessment and have probably been the main route for the training of assessors. However, such courses have an appendage-like quality and can divorce assessment skills from clinical and teaching skills with which they are integrated. Where opportunities and resources for continuing education are scarce and a coherent strategy for comprehensive professional development has not been developed, such courses may be the only means of developing assessment skills.

Assessing assessment skills

Teaching can be a solitary experience in the sense that, once qualified, teachers may receive little or no critical appraisal based on the direct observation of peers. This may be because opportunities are not available or, simply, that these are avoided. Consequently, innovation and excellence are not identified; nor is poor performance. The same observation can be true of assessors; as an issue of personal and professional development it is important that assessors should be able to receive sensitive and helpful feedback on their assessment skills. There are a variety of approaches to assessing assessors; probably the least helpful is the 'formal' examination of an assessor whilst assessing. A system of periodic peer review and self-assessment, where a colleague observes the practice of an assessor and then acts as a facilitator for self-assessment, is particularly useful. Additionally, meetings of assessors that have the characteristics of a 'support group' rather than a formal committee enable colleagues to discuss developments in assessment strategy and to share individual and collective concerns about assessment. These may include the presentation of current 'case histories' in assessment. This provides a focus on what is really happening rather than a theorised discussion on assessment principles.

Table 5.1 Summary of advantages and disadvantages of non-clinical assessment methods

Method	Advantages	Disadvantages
Timed unseen essay examination	Assessment of sophisticated cognitive abilities. Inference of skills and attitudes. Easy to set	Unseen examinations tend to measure relatively simple abilities such as recognition and memory of facts. Giving students notice of the questions eliminates 'question spotting' or permitting students access to reference material during the examination enables markers to increase the allocation of marks to higher cognitive skills. Timed examinations favour students who can write quickly — writing speed is unlikely to be an objective of the course. A choice of questions, though increasing the coverage of the syllabus, means that students can be taking 'different' examinations. Despite 'marking criteria', variations in marks are awarded by different examiners.
Short-answer tests	Assessment of knowledge of information and appreciation of principles. Broader coverage of syllabus. 'Tighter' criteria for marking and increasing inter-marker reliability. Easy to set.	Limited scope to demonstrate creativity, originality and problem-solving skills.

Method	Advantages	Disadvantages
Objective tests (various types)	Assessment of a broad range of mental abilities. Comprehensive syllabus coverage. 'Absolute' marking criteria — response is unequivocally right or wrong. A bank of questions, once established, can be used repeatedly, permitting useful statistical comparisons between courses/students. Easy to mark. Rapid knowledge of overall results. Can be self-administered by students. Particularly useful when applied to computer-assisted learning programmes.	Construction of valid items is notoriously difficult. Many important issues of assessment require explanation and qualification — there is no absolutely right or wrong answer. Permit guessing although this can be discouraged by negative marking, i.e. marks being deducted for wrong answers. Difficult to provide students with detailed feedback on each individual item.
Clinical case histories	Directly relate knowledge base to clinical practice. Comprehensive and integrated syllabus coverage.	Problems associated with confidentiality and disclosure of personal information. May reflect standards of desirable care, rather than actual care delivered. Difficult to grade.
Project and small-scale research	Assess skills of active enquiry, information retrieval, hypothesis-testing, problem-solving and critical analysis. Organisation and presentation skills.	'Loose' marking criteria. Time and effort involved might be disproportionate relative to other assessed work.
Simulations	Assessment of specific skills. Convenient, predictable and controlled. Safe.	Perceived as 'artificial' by participants with consequences for performance. Indirect evidence of actual skills level in 'real' situation.
Viva voce group discussions	Assessment of presentation and interpersonal skills. Reasoning and debating abilities.	Favours students with good verbal facility. Requires exceptional examiner skills.

Non-clinical methods of assessment

The relative advantages and disadvantages of a range of non-clinical assessment methods are summarised in Table 5.1.

References

Ball J et al (1983) Monitor. Newcastle upon Tyne: Polytechnic Products Limited
Beattie A & Bessent M (1986) Blueprint for the Future. London: King's Fund
Bligh D (1975) Teaching Students Exeter: U E T S
Department of Health & Social Security (1983) Nurses, Midwives and Health Visitors Rules Approval Order 1983 (Cmd 873) London: HMSO.
English National Board (1986) Guidelines to Preparing Continuous Assessment (86/16). London: E N B
Joint Board of Clinical Nursing Studies (1983) The Teaching Objective in Postbasic Clinical Studies Outline Curricula, Occasional Publication 5. London: J B C N S
Kelly G (1955) The Psychology of Personal Constructs, Vols 1–2. Norton
King Edward's Hospital Fund (1972) Assessment. London: K E H F
Law B (1984) Uses and Abuses of Profiling. London: Harper & Row
McHale M (1985) The importance of awareness. Nursing Mirror, **161**(18), 30–31
Nicklin P (1984) A Description of Personal Construct Theory and Its Potential Application by the Nurse Teacher. Unpublished M Ed assignment, University of Nottingham
Pope M (1978) Monitoring and reflecting in teacher training. In Personal Construct Psychology. New York: Academic Press
Steinaker N W & Bell M R (1979) The Experiential Taxonomy, pp 53–54. London: Academic Press
U M I S T (1985) What the Patient Thinks. Manchester: Department of Management Sciences
United Kingdom Central Council (1984) Code of Professional Conduct, 2nd ed. London: U K C C
Wandelt M & Slater D (1975) Nursing Competences Rating Scale. New York: Appleton-Century-Crofts

6
The Learning Environment

The concept of 'learning environment' is a relatively recent addition to the vocabulary of nurse education. Although the notion that particular conditions or circumstances enhance or inhibit learning is not new, it is within the last decade that the scientific scrutiny of the millieu in which nurse training takes place has gained momentum. In particular, the research of Orton (1981), Fretwell (1982) and Ogier (1982, 1986) illuminates the characteristics of wards that provide a positive 'learning environment', and confirms the crucial role of the ward sister in creating a climate that is conducive to learning. In this chapter 'the learning environment' will be construed as those circumstances that directly or otherwise influence the teaching and learning of nursing. This deliberately loose definition, whilst embracing clinical experience, will permit discussion of other factors that influence the education of student nurses.

Creating the environment – the curriculum development team

Fundamental to the responsibilities of the curriculum development team (C D T) is creating and nurturing an environment in which the curriculum will thrive. For this to be achieved, the C D T must have not only a coherent philosophy and unambiguous terms of reference but a common perception of what is meant by the term 'curriculum'. Quinn (1980) favours Nicholls and Nicholls' (1978) definition: 'Curriculum is all the opportunities planned for pupils by teachers.' This is a comprehensive description that is seriously flawed. 'Planned for pupils by teachers' appears to cast 'pupils' in the role of passive if not docile recipients, and further implies that curriculum planning is the exclusive responsibility of teachers. The membership of the C D T should extend to all disciplines and professions that have a legitimate interest in the course, not least the students. Further, the discrepancy between what is taught and what is practised can only be widened if curriculum planning and development is perceived as a teacher-dominated theoretical and academic exercise. A more useful description of curriculum is: 'A curriculum is an attempt to communicate the essential features of an educational proposal in such a form that it is open to critical scrutiny and capable of effective translation into practice' (Stenhouse 1975). The issue of evaluation will be considered in detail in Chapter 9; however, at this stage it is appropriate to discuss how the 'learning environment' can be scrutinised by the C D T. Such scrutiny or 'auditing' has the following purposes:

— Identification of clinical placements for inclusion in a scheme of training
— Identification of exceptional practice – providing an exemplar for other wards or units
— Diagnosis of problems within the learning environment that require remedial action
— Exclusion of clinical areas that do not provide a positive learning environment

The auditing of the learning environment has always been a feature of approval visits by the statutory authority. Previously, there has possibly been a tendency on the occasion of such inspections for the school or institution to maximise the strengths of the learning environment and minimise or attempt to conceal the weaknesses and deficiencies. Clearly, a more professional and responsible approach is for the school and its C D T to employ an open system of auditing, the results of which are made available to clinicians, managers and teachers as well as to the officers of the National Board. Elliot and Adelman (1974) suggest that 'the whole idea of self-criticism and self-monitoring is threatening to many teachers; the organisational set-up in many schools does not help teachers to engage in this kind of self-appraisal and many teachers find it difficult to discuss their problems with their colleagues'. In the previous chapter 'self and peer' assessment was advocated for students. It would be patently inconsistent if this value did not equally apply to the curriculum development team and the learning environment it is responsible for creating.

Characteristics of a learning environment

Fretwell (1980, 1982) concluded that many factors contribute to the ward learning environment and summarised them in Fig. 6.1.

From this evidence the curriculum development team can construct a standardised instrument to audit the ward/clinical environment. This may be in the form of a checklist, questionnaire or rating scale. Figure 6.2 is a specimen of an auditing instrument. It is open to criticism, and the reader may identify important areas that are omitted or, conversely, note elements that appear to be trivial. What is important is that the instrument is of local design and in this respect 'owned' by the C D T, and as such reflects the values and beliefs of those developing the curriculum.

Auditing of the learning environment should be undertaken at regular intervals; this may be annually or whenever the circumstances of the ward change. Such circumstances would include a change of ward management or an alteration of its clinical function. As new clinical services are developed a base-line audit should be performed. Occasionally, a particular ward or department may consistently be poorly rated by students; alternatively, a specific clinical area may have a sustained high absence and sickness rate — in these

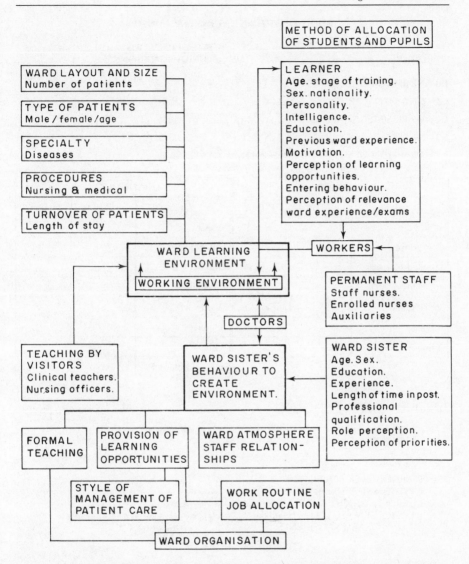

Fig. 6.1   Characteristics of a learning environment (Fretwell 1976). (Source: *An Inquiry into the Ward Learning Environment* (1980) and *Ward Teaching and Learning* (1982), Joan E Fretwell. © Crown Copyright, reprinted by permission of the DHSS and the author)

circumstances an audit may be undertaken for diagnostic reasons. It has been suggested that 'self-criticism and self-monitoring' are potentially threatening; consequently the C D T should ensure that ward sisters are appropriately trained to audit their wards (the issue of training will be developed later in this chapter). An audit of the ward learning environment is undertaken by the ward sister, a

AUDIT OF STUDENT NURSE PLACEMENTS

DATE AUDIT COMPLETED:............................. DATE OF PREVIOUS AUDIT:....................
WARD/DEPT:...................................... SPECIALITY/DESIGNATION:...........................

1:0   NURSING ESTABLISHMENT

1:1   UNIT MANAGER:...

1:2   WARD SISTER/CHARGE SISTER..

1:3   NURSE TEACHER: ....

1:4   PROFILE OF STAFFING ESTABLISHMENT

DAY DUTY			NIGHT DUTY		
Grade	F/Time	P/Time	Grade	F/Time	P/Time
WS/CN			WS/CN		
Staff Nurse			Staff Nurse		
Enrolled Nurse			Enrolled Nurse		
Auxiliaries			Auxiliaries		
Ward Clerk			Ward Clerk		
(Other)			(Other)		
(Other)			(Other)		
			Internal Rotation	Yes/No	

1:5   DUTY HOURS OF F/TIME STAFF

A.M.   From .... To ....
P.M.   From .... To ....
Night Duty From .... To ....

1:6   LEARNER ALLOCATION
OPTIMUM STUDENT ALLOCATION:...
CURRENT STUDENT ALLOCATION:...
RATIO OF TRAINED STAFF : LEARNERS: ....
MEAN % OF ABSENCE/SICKNESS:...

2:0   WARD/UNIT ACTIVITY

2:1   NUMBER OF BEDS:..
2:2   NUMBER OF ADMISSIONS pa.:...
2:3   MEAN % OF OCCUPANCY:..
2:4   MEAN STAY:..........DAYS
2:5   SEX OF PATIENT/CLIENT: ....
2:6   NUMBER OF CONSULTANTS: ....
2:7   NUMBER OF OUTPATIENTS (RESIDENTS) pa.: ....
2:8   NUMBER OF DAY CASES pa.:..

3:0   NURSING STAFF PROFILE

Name	Grade	Professional Qualifications	Postbasic Cont. Ed. Courses	Assessor

4:0   COMMUNICATIONS

4:1   THE FOLLOWING ARE AVAILABLE AND USED

(a)	Operational Policy Folder	Yes/No
(b)	Current Clinical Procedures	Yes/No
(c)	U K C C Code of Professional Conduct	Yes/No
(d)	Ward Learning Objectives	Yes/No

4:2   THE FOLLOWING MINUTES/INFORMATION IS RECEIVED AND AVAILABLE TO ALL STAFF

(a)	Unit Meetings	Yes/No
(b)	Assessors' Meetings	Yes/No
(c)	Curriculum Development Team Meetings	Yes/No
(d)	Services Update Bulletins	Yes/No
(e)	Audit of Clinical Placement	Yes/No
(f)		Yes/No

The following criteria items are considered to be significant in providing an environment that is conducive to learning:

Each should be evaluated as:

A – GOOD   B – ACCEPTABLE   C – UNSATISFACTORY

5:0   LEARNING CLIMATE

		Comments	A	B	C
5:1	The experience offered is congruent with identified learning objectives				
5:2	Clinical practices are consistent with Unit/District Policies/Guidelines				
5:3	There is evidence of multi-disciplinary approaches to care				
5:4	Off-duty is available well in advance — trained staff supervision is planned/mentors are known to students				
5:5	There is evidence of continuity of care — trained staff are rarely moved to other wards/departments				
5:6	Student abilities are considered so that excessive responsibilities or failure to learn is avoided				
5:7	An extended teaching report is part of the established ward/department routine				
5:8	Medical and other disciplines demonstrate active involvement in teaching students				
5:9	A named and described model of care is employed				
5:10	Nursing care is planned subsequent to assessment and declared nursing objectives to meet patients/residents needs				
5:11	There is evidence that care plans directly influence delivery of care				

6:0   MENTORS/ROLE/MODELS

		Comments	A	B	C
6:1	Trained staff levels permit appropriate levels of supervision				
6:2	Trained staff have a clear understanding of their educational role				
6:3	Attitudes towards students are positive				
6:4	All staff have access to planned programmes of continuing education				
6:5	Assessors receive adequate support and guidance for their role				
6:6	Staff demonstrate a commitment to their own professional development				

6:0   MENTORS/ROLE/MODELS

		Comments	A	B	C
6:7	Learners receive an appropriate induction and orientation to the ward				
6:8	Learners receive intermediate and final reports as required by the curriculum				
6:9	There is evidence that students receive appropriate support, guidance and counselling				
6:10	There is evidence of effective relationships with teaching staff, in particular the teacher responsible for the ward/department				
6:11	A 'resource area' is available with relevant journals/articles, etc.				

7:0   TEACHING STAFF

		Comments	A	B	C
7:1	Teachers visit the ward/department on a regular planned basis and work as a member of the ward/department team				
7:2	Teachers assist clinical/care staff in the formulation of learning objectives that are regularly revised				
7:3	Teachers participate in unit meetings				
7:4	Teachers contribute to the role development of trained staff				

8:0   STUDENTS

		Comments	A	B	C
8:1	Students express positive attitudes when evaluating this placement				
8:2	Students consistently achieve the learning objectives of this placement				
8:3	Students are adequately supervised by trained staff				
8:4	Students receive adequate support and tuition from teaching staff				

9:0 PHYSICAL ENVIRONMENT

		Comments	A	B	C
9:1	The ward/department environment is appropriate and equipped for its designated function				
9:2	There is adequate storage space				
9:3	The Health and Safety Policy is complied with				
9:4	Facilities/amenities ensure privacy for patients/residents				
9:5	Equipment is maintained in a safe working order				
9:6	Staff facilities: office accommodation/changing facilities are adequate				

10:0 AUDIT SUMMARY

The ward is suitable/unsuitable for inclusion in the circuit of educational placements for student nurses. The following recommendations are made:

....
Chairman of Evaluation and   Ward Sister/Charge Nurse/
Monitoring Team/Curriculum   Head of Department
Development Team

Date: ....   Date: ....

Fig. 6.2   Ward learning environment — audit

nurse teacher and a member of the C D T. A logical development of this type of audit is peer review, where a sister or charge nurse from another ward joins the audit team. This is a particularly useful method of not only monitoring clinical and educational activities but also of disseminating good practices from one clinical area to another.

By logical extension, 'peer review' can be extended further. E N B Circular 85/30/MAT (April 1985) advises that: 'During consideration of a policy for the future, the Board (E N B) agreed that certain principles would be adopted including . . . (v) Peer group review of courses.'

Evaluation and audit of nursing curricula is currently undertaken internally both by the appropriate C D T of the training institution and by the National Board. The training institution is neither impartial nor independent, which has implications for the quality of evaluative judgements. The officers of the National Board, whilst impartial, are clearly not independent of the training institution as they directly influence curriculum design and development and, ultimately, formally present the curriculum to the Board's Approvals Committee. Kenworthy and Nicklin (1987) describe a system of peer audit between two schools of nursing and assert that the strength of the system is not only that evaluation and audit from another institution is both impartial and independent but it is based on the judgements of practising clinical nurses and teachers. This is not viewed as an alternative to current practice but as an adjunct to it.

The ward sister and the learning environment

Fretwell (1982) concludes:

> 'Results show that it is not enough to allocate student or pupil nurses to a ward to do the work, for if nothing is done to integrate learners into the ward team, learning will be minimal. . . . A conscious effort is needed to change a working environment into a learning environment. The key to change is the ward sister.'

However, the role of the ward sister, what with changes in clinical nursing practice, advances in technology, developments in nurse education and reform of management arrangements, has become an increasingly complex undertaking. It is self-evident that a basic three-year nurse training course inadequately prepares the newly registered nurse for the role of staff nurse (D H S S 1982, 1986), let alone that of ward sister. This is not a contemporary perception:

> 'Every ward sister should attend a course on the psychology of teaching . . . ' (Horder Report, in Royal College of Nursing 1943).

> 'The particular problems of providing suitable "post graduate" preparation for ward sisters requires special consideration. We suggest that the content of such a course might include principles and methods of teaching . . . ' (Wood Report, in Ministry of Health 1947).

An important initiative in the development and research of ward sister training has been undertaken by the King's Fund (D H S S 1984). Nationally, a variety of programmes for ward sisters, or staff nurses aspiring to the role of ward sister, have been developed. A common feature of these schemes is that they are ward-based and employ a preceptor or mentor system where the 'trainee' can observe, analyse and criticise a competent role model:

> 'The best and quickest method for preparation (of ward sisters) is in the real life situation; where the nurse will encounter the day to day problems and challenges of running a ward, but will have the advantage of the support of a tutor to guide her studies and an experienced ward sister to act as a role model' (Davies 1981).

The evaluation of such courses is most encouraging; however, the opportunity to undertake such preparation may elude the majority of ward sisters. Alternative strategies of role development can include utilisation of 'freestanding' courses

such as E N B Course 998 'Teaching and Assessing in Clinical Practice', the City
and Guilds Further Education Certificate (730) and the Open University Course
P553 (Nursing Process), combined with locally devised units of learning focusing
on such skills as 'personnel management', 'research appreciation and application', 'clinical budgeting', 'ward management' and similar units that reflect
locally identified skills requirements.

Earlier in this chapter the discrepancy between what is taught and what is
practised was referred to; clearly, such discrepancies have implications for the
quality of the learning environment. One approach to achieving a closer
integration between theory and practice has been through joint clinical teaching
appointments, the fundamental assumption being that the clinical learning
environment can be substantially enhanced if those with clinical authority also
have the education and training of students as a primary concern. The King's
Fund Report (1985) on joint clinical–teaching appointments in nursing concludes: 'Joint appointees, as far as they are able, want to teach about the nursing
they practise and want to practise the kind of nursing they teach.' There can be
little doubt that joint charge nurse/tutor appointments have improved the clinical
learning environment. However, this success has possibly owed more to the
commitment and abilities of the individual appointees than the appointment
itself. Simultaneously reconciling the conflicts and pressures of being a ward
sister and a nurse tutor is patently stressful and requires individuals of exceptional
calibre: 'Perhaps it is because joint appointments are so complex and demanding that there are so few of them' (King's Fund 1985). Consequently, joint
appointments are possibly best perceived as an important but limited strategy for
enriching the learning climate. What is certain is that the ward sister is the single
most important person in creating a learning environment. Ogier (1982, 1986)
identifies attributes that discriminate between the 'ideal' and 'non-ideal' sister,
based on student's responses:

— Sister makes sure I know what to do.
— Sister makes sure I know how to do what she asks.
— When I don't know something, sister makes sure she (or someone) tells me
   how to do it or find out about it.
— When I'm worried or don't know something I feel I can go to ask sister.
— Sister makes sure each learner gets a fair share of any learning opportunities.
— I feel I can talk to sister.
— Sister is interested in me.
— Sister is helpful to me.

Continuing education and training in the learning environment

The continuing professional development of nurses has been, and remains in
many instances, sporadic and fragmented. Opportunities for continuing education vary dramatically from district to district. It is an indictment to the service that
sustaining and developing nursing skills is dependent on the whim of the
individual nurse or health district that employs her. A sustained criticism of nurse
education has been that, not infrequently, students in the final phase of their

training, although less skilled than their registered mentors, are probably more knowledgeable. This, despite a professional code of conduct (U K C C 1984) that explicitly requires that each registered nurse ' . . . take every reasonable opportunity to maintain and improve professional knowledge and competence . . . and, in the context of the individual's own knowledge and experience and sphere of authority, assist peers and subordinates to develop professional competence in accordance with their needs'.

An essential prerequisite of a positive learning environment is that all registered nurses should maintain and develop their skills. During 1987 the U K C C (1987a) introduced a system of periodic registration and has subsequently commenced formal consultation with nurses and their employers to determine how 'mandatory periodic refreshment' should be linked to registration, with nurses at the time of receiving their registration being required to demonstrate evidence of further training. Additionally, the Council, in its Project 2000 final proposals (1987b), expresses its commitment to improving the education and training environment and proposes that practitioners be given formal preparation for their training and educational roles in practice settings.

The continuing professional development of the registered nurse is not exclusively the responsibility of the individual or the employing authority, but of both. The individual nurse has a right to expect the provision of training opportunities and the employer should expect the nurse to maintain and develop the skills for which she is employed. This should not be a tacit agreement but a formal contractual obligation. The provision of an apposite and comprehensive continuing education programme requires not only the direct funding of teaching staff but additionally manpower planning needs to take account of the 'time lost' to training. There is little point in making a training provision to which nurses cannot be released due to shortage of staff.

> 'But I well recognise the ambivalence of the nurse manager. Releasing staff for training can overload slender staff resources; in contrast, not to release staff for training discourages nursing skills development. Faced with this dilemma, a manager may well ask if she is more likely to be criticised for being short of staff or short of skills. I suggest it would be the former' (Nicklin 1985).

However, training should not be considered as being synonymous with absence from the work place. Indeed, a reasonable criticism of much training is that it is unreal, synthetic or an academic simulation.

> The evaluation project clearly showed the need for more comprehensive provision of education and support for all trained nursing staff. . . . This does not necessarily mean the provision of more courses, which have costs in terms of per capita expenditure and loss of service time, and may be insufficiently integrated with ward work to be of great value.' (D H S S 1986).

There is much potential for the further development of 'role-based' training and 'distance learning' as components of a strategy of continuing education for nurses. A comprehensive strategy for continuing education and professional development is described by the Scottish Home and Health Department (1981).

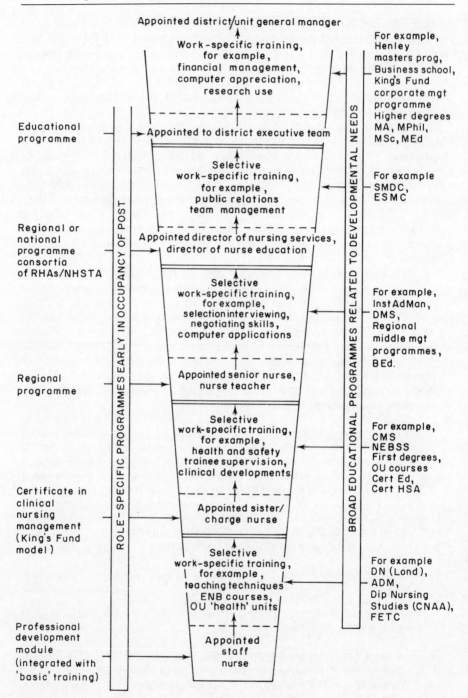

Fig. 6.3 A strategy for continuing education. Scottish Home and Health Department (1981)

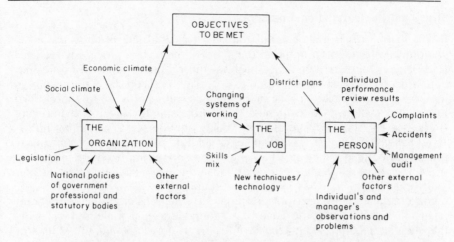

Fig. 6.4   Factors influencing the organisation of continuing education programmes. (Source: National Staff Committee for Nurses and Midwives (1981). *The Organisation and Provision of Continuing In-service Education and Training.* © Crown Copyright, reproduction by permission of the NHS Training Authority)

This combines both 'role-based' training focusing on the skills required in the current post and 'broad-based' programmes related to individual development needs (Fig. 6.3).

In concluding this section on continuing education as a prerequisite of a positive learning environment, it is necessary to consider briefly the identification of training needs. Nursing skills should positively correlate with the demands being made on the service. By logical extension, the training and retraining of nurses should relate directly to the needs of the client/patient population. If this assertion is reasonable, the focus of training should be a template for the focus of nursing care. However, scrutiny of continuing education programmes often more accurately reflects the aspirations and interests of nurses rather than the needs of priority client care groups. Accurate and detailed identification of training needs is best achieved through a sensitive system of performance review, where the skills of the individual and the nursing team are matched against the objectives of the ward or department. The factors that influence the organisation of continuing education programmes are illustrated in Fig. 6.4.

Nursing and therefore nurse education competes with other disciplines and services within the N H S for resources; in this respect, demand will always exceed supply. Consequently, it is essential that continuing education should demonstrate that it represents 'value for money'. There is a need to generate 'performance indicators' that demonstrate this. Activity data, such as the number of courses or participants, are insufficient; what is required are data that demonstrate that the quality of care and the quality of the learning environment are improved as a consequence of continuing education. This is a fertile area for further research and development.

Stress and the learning environment

In 1975, John Birch speculated that anxiety was a significant influence in the withdrawal of students from nurse training. Fourteen years previously Menzies (1961) had expressed her concern about the problems of stress in nursing. Subsequently, the literature devoted to occupation-related stress among nurses has grown substantially. In spite of this, Hingley and Harris (1986) report: 'We believe the level of stress awareness in the profession is low rather than seeing stress as a solvable problem. The prevailing attitude seems to be that nurses should either put up with the difficulties or get out.' Nurses confront suffering as few other people do; they are often expected to do the impossible in the way of providing comfort and care. Nursing is located within a large bureaucratic and rigid organisation that has lacked the security of an established and stable management structure for over a decade. Nursing transmits a culture of compliance — consequently, the nurse may set unrealistic goals for herself, believing that she can accomplish an activity or feat in an unrealistic amount of time or against insurmountable odds. With respect to patient care, nurses expect themselves to be all things to all people, and then chastise themselves when they fall short. The discrepancies between the values and behaviours learned in the school of nursing and those required in the work situation are well known. This gulf between what is theorised and what is practised is a major source of stress for nurses. The student nurse is located in the midst of this perceptual conflict, attempting to make sense of her emerging nursing identity — no mean feat when one considers that the majority of students are adolescent and seeking to establish their own individual identity.

In 1978, Shubin applied the term 'burn-out' to a syndrome promoted by job-related distress in nursing, the characteristics of burn-out being physical and emotional exhaustion, involving the development of negative self-concept, negative job attitudes and a loss of concern and feeling for clients. 'Stress' has a contemporary popularity amongst the ordinary public, educationalists and helping professions; it is possible to speculate that the phenomenon of 'burn-out' is more apparent than real and simply promoted by the 'bandwagon' effect! Certainly, it is difficult to produce direct and objective evidence of burn-out. Burn-out is analogous to 'shell shock' or 'battle fatigue'; for many nurses to admit to burn-out would be synonymous with 'lacking moral fibre' and would offend the characteristic British solution to stress — the 'stiff upper lip'. Chambers-Clark (1980) describes a reluctance among nurses to legitimise their own right to health and well-being. This legitimisation may well conflict with meeting the emotional demands of patients and subordinates. Despite the difficulties in directly quantifying the incidence of occupationally related stress, Nicklin (1987) and Hingley et al (1986) quite independently identified that workload, quality of relationships and conflicts and ambiguities of nursing roles were a significant source of stress. The majority of respondents in both studies considered nursing to be increasingly stressful.

Preventing burn-out is infinitely preferable to treating it. Nurses are the Health Service's most costly resource. The cost of stress-related illness, absenteeism and inefficiency is a major drain on limited N H S resources. According to Cooper

(1981), 'For the country's employers of manpower stress has its costs . . . stress related illnesses are second and third in those reasons for short term sickness absence.' Strategies for the prevention of stress can be classified as organisational and personal. While the organisation most certainly has a responsibility for diminishing stress, each nurse has an individual responsibility to prevent burn-out in herself. There is an inescapable paradox that stress to one nurse is satisfaction to another. Lazarus (1967) has demonstrated that a stressful situation cannot be defined by reference to objective criteria. Only the individual nurse can define her own stress. Nicklin's (1984) research reveals a paucity of provision by health districts in preventing occupationally related stress among nurses:

> 'The responsibility for maintaining health should be a reflection of the basic relationship between the individual and the organisation. . . . There is only limited evidence of managerial and organisational methods being employed to combat stress. Though disturbing it is somewhat predictable that "the cobbler's children are worst shod".'

Asa Briggs, as Chairman of the Committee on Nursing (D H S S 1972), was impressed by the stressors of nursing: 'We have been struck by the powers of the pressures on the nurses . . . given the highly demanding work and profound and unpredictable pressures.' Briggs identified 'the creation of a comprehensive counselling service as an urgent top priority'. Fifteen years later, only a handful of counsellors conforming to Briggs' recommendations are employed by the N H S. Some health districts are adopting health promotion policies that encourage employees to stop smoking, discourage the abuse of alcohol and advocate regular exercise and a 'healthy' diet. Such approaches are clearly welcomed but have a tendency to treat the overt symptoms of stress rather than addressing the underlying problem. Seyle (1956) suggests that individuals should develop a code of 'altruistic egoism' — a time-honoured procedure for managing stress — none of us can expect others to look after us more than after themselves! What is implied here is that individuals must accept responsibility for themselves. Birch's (1978) research revealed: 'The sample of students and pupils in this study emerges as a relatively anxiety-ridden group.' Birch concluded that a reform of the curriculum was required to provide students with the skills to meet patients' psychological needs. It is also apparent that whilst enabling students to meet the psychological needs of their patients there is an urgent requirement that students should possess the skills to meet their own psychological needs. Clearly this assertion does not apply exclusively to students. As a contribution to curriculum building and the development of a 'healthy' learning environment, both basic and postbasic courses should include self-management skills that will prevent occupationally related stress. Techniques such as progressive relaxation, self-awareness, aerobics, assertion training and guided imagery have a legitimate place in health-based curricula. In the previous section, continuing education was described as a prerequisite of a positive learning environment; it should also be perceived as a method of preventing stress. Because a discrepancy between what is expected from self and others and the individual's current level of

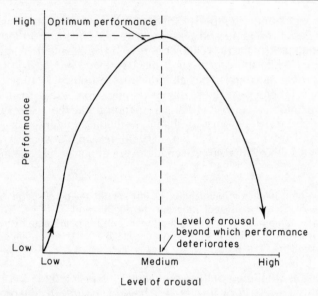

Fig. 6.5   Yerkes Dodson law — relationship between arousal and performance

knowledge and competence can be stressful, continuing professional education can be perceived not only as a service enhancing necessity but also a method of diminishing occupationally related stress. Ford (1983) describes a scheme of orientation and continuing education specifically aimed at reducing nursing staff stress.

Of the range of potentially useful stress-reducing activities, support groups appear to have gained the greatest degree of acceptance in this country. Firth (1984) considers that personal support is just as important as adequate staffing. Mastach (1978) writes:

> 'Burnout rates are lower for those professions who actively express, analyse and share their personal feelings with colleagues. Not only do they get things off their chest but have an opportunity to receive constructive feedback from other people and to develop new perspectives of their relationships.'

Earlier in this chapter role-based training utilising preceptors or mentors was discussed. Hingley and Harris (1986) advise: 'We believe that *all* nurses should have access to a professional supervisor or mentor, someone within the workplace who can listen openly, challenge constructively and guide supportively.' In Chapter 9 the skills of listening and responding are considered in detail.

Prophit (1981) reports that studies in longevity have cited two primary sociopsychological measures that are more predictive of long life than any other; work satisfaction and overall happiness. Yet work is a two-edged sword; it has the potential to enrich life but also the potential to create stress and suffering. The hypothetical relationship between arousal and performance is well known (Fig.

6.5). Arousal is essential for optimum performance, including learning; however, as stress mounts performance deteriorates.

The strength and success of curriculum delivery in nurse education is directly dependent on the environment in which learning and teaching takes place. It has been suggested that nurse education, metaphorically speaking, is poised on the San Andreas Fault. The tensions between service delivery and educational intent have the potential to erupt, causing chaos and disruption. With or without Project 2000, students require the freedom to learn from competent role models in a stimulating and supportive environment where there is close proximity between nursing theory and nursing practice.

References

Birch J A (1975) *To Nurse or Not to Nurse*. London: R C N

Birch J A (1978) *Anxiety in Nurse Education*. Unpublished Ph D thesis, University of Newcastle upon Tyne

Chambers-Clark C (1980) Burnout – assessment and intervention. *Journal of Nursing Administration*, **9**, 49–43

Cooper C (1981) *The Stress Check*. Englewood Cliffs, N J: Prentice Hall

Davies C (1981) Training for ward sisters. An innovative research and development project. *Nurse Education Today*, **1**(2)

Department of Health & Social Security (1972) *Report of the Committee on Nursing (Briggs Report)*. London: H M S O

Department of Health & Social Security (1982) *Professional Development in Clinical Nursing: The 1980s Seminar Report*. London: D H S S

Department of Health & Social Security (1984) *The Ward Sister Training Project*. London: N E R U, Chelsea College

Department of Health & Social Security (1986) *Professional Development Schemes for Newly Registered Nurses. Evaluation – Summary of Findings*. London: D H S S

Elliot J & Adelman C (1974) *Innovation in Teaching and Action Research*. Norwich: Centre for Applied Research in Education

English National Board (1985) *Approved Process for Conversion Nursing, Midwifery and Health Visiting (85/30/MAT)*. London: E N B

Firth H (1984) Sources of good staff support. *Nursing Times*, **80**(18)

Ford R (1983) Reducing nursing-staff stress through scheduling, orientation and continuing education. *Nurs. Clin. Nurse Am.*, **18**(3)

Fretwell J E (1982) *Ward Teaching and Learning*. London: R C N

Hingley P & Harris P (1986) Lowering the tension. *Nursing Times*, **83**(32), 52–53

Hingley P *et al* (1986) *Stress in Nurse Managers*, Project Paper 60. London: King's Fund Centre

Kenworthy N & Nicklin P J Educational audit. *Senior Nurse*, **7**(1), 22–24 (1987)

King's Fund (1985) *Joint Clinical-Teaching Appointments*, Project Paper 51. London: King's Fund Centre

Lazarus R (1967) *Cognitive and Personality Factors Underlying Threat and Coping in Psychological Stress*. East Norwalk, C T: Appleton-Century-Crofts

Mastach C (1978) Job burnout – how people cope. *Public Welfare*, Spring

Menzies I P H (1961) *The Functioning of Social System as a Defence against Anxiety*. London: Tavistock Publications

Ministry of Health (1947) *Report after Working Party on the Recruitment and Training of Nurses (Wood Report)* London: H M S O

Nicholls A & Nicholls H (1978) *Developing a Curriculum*. London: Allen & Unwin

Nicklin P J (1984) *Organisational Management of Nursing Related Stress in one N H S Region*. Unpublished M Ed assignment, University of Nottingham

Nicklin P J (1985) A case of mistaken responsibility. *Nursing Mirror*, **160**(19), 26–28

Nicklin P J (1987) Violence to the spirit. *Senior Nurse*, **6**(5), 10–12

N S C (N & M) (1981) *Recommendations on the Organisation and Provision of Continuing In-service Education.*

Ogier M E (1982) *An Ideal Ward Sister?* London: R C N

Ogier M E (1986) An 'ideal' ward sister – seven years on. *Nursing Times*, **82**(2), 54–57

Orton H D (1981) *Ward Learning Climate*. London: R C N

Prophit P (1981) Burnout: the cost of involvement of being human in the helping professions. In *Research: A Base for the Future*. University of Edinburgh

Quinn F M (1980) *The Principles and Practice of Nurse Education*. London: Croom Helm

Royal College of Nursing (1943) *Report of the Nursing Reconstruction Committee (Horder Report)* London: R C N

Scottish Home & Health Department (1981) *Continuing Education for the Nursing Profession in Scotland*. Edinburgh: S H H D

Seyle H (1956) *The Stress of Life*. Maidenhead: McGraw-Hill

Shubin S (1978) Burnout, the professional hazard in nursing. *Nursing*, **8**(7), 22–27

Stenhouse L (1975) *A Introduction to Curriculum Research and Development*. London: Heinemann

United Kingdom Central Council (1984) *Code of Professional Conduct*. London: U K C C

United Kingdom Central Council (1987a) *Mandatory Periodic Refreshment for Nurses and Health Visitors – Discussion Paper*. London: U K C C

United Kingdom Central Council (1987b) *Project 2000: The Final Proposals*, Project Paper 9. London: U K C C

7
An Introduction to Counselling and Counselling Skills

The focus of this chapter is concerned with the skills of *helping others to understand themselves better and enabling them to be more effective in solving their problems*. Although these skills will be discussed in the context of helping students, the principles are just as applicable to helping relationships with patients, colleagues and friends. Many student nurses are away from home for the first time and are in the process of resolving the normal emotional and social conflicts of adolescence and early adulthood. They are subjected to the rigours of study and anxieties of examinations, in addition to experiencing at first hand the suffering and anguish of others. Unusual demands for pity, compassion and patience are made on students who may have inadequate experience or skills to cope with them. It is hardly surprising that students encounter problem situations with which they require sensitive and skilled assistance. But who should assist? Helping and counselling are not the exclusive responsibility of those formally called and employed as counsellors; in this respect the Standing Conference for the Advancement of Counselling (SCAC) (1977) identifies three groups of helpers:

1 People who are employed specifically as counsellors — referred to as 'professional counsellors'
2 People for whom counselling is a legitimate and generally recognised, if subordinate, part of their role — referred to as 'counsellors'
3 People who use counselling skills in the normal course of their working lives, possibly without recognising them as such — referred to as 'doing counselling' but not as being counsellors

Asa Briggs, Chairman of the Committee on Nursing (1972), expressed concern about the stresses of nursing and identified 'the creation of a comprehensive counselling service as an urgent top priority'. The reality, over fifteen years later, is that there are less than a handful of trained counsellors employed exclusively to provide a comprehensive counselling service to nurses and nurse students.

93

However, even if the service that Briggs envisaged existed today, students would still require the helping skills of their qualified colleagues. In the absence of such a service the basic skills of 'doing counselling' are even more necessary and fundamental to the trained nursing role (Nicklin 1987). Such skills are implied by the U K C C Code of Professional Conduct (1984):

> 'Each registered nurse, midwife and health visitor is accountable for his or her practice, and, in the exercise of professional accountability shall . . .
> (ii)   Have regard for the workload of, and the pressures on, professional colleagues and subordinates and take appropriate action if these are seen to be such as to constitute abuse of the individual practitioner and/or jeopardise safe standards of practice.'

Therefore, the purpose of this chapter is to enable trained nurses to reflect on their 'helping' or 'doing counselling' skills and, where appropriate, to encourage further skills practice to improve their counselling performance. The words of the previous sentence were carefully chosen, 'to enable', 'to reflect', 'to encourage', 'to improve' — the reason for this is that whilst most people would not expect to be able to drive a car without training and practice, many individuals feel that interpersonal or 'people skills' should come naturally, and therefore the suggestion of training in this area is a criticism of their personal qualities. Conversely, training is considered to be some sort of remote and mystical process for a selected few. The evidence is that basic and effective helping skills can be substantially improved through training and practice and that these fundamental skills of helping can be developed by the average, healthy and caring individual. Of this situation, Egan (1986) advises:

> 'Helping is never neutral, that is, it is always "for better or for worse". Helping is a powerful process that is all too easy to mismanage. Unskilled and mismanaged helping can do a great deal of harm but skilled and socially intelligent workers can do a great deal of good.'

Counselling theory and principles

Like other nursing activities, counselling is essentially a practical activity and in the past there has possibly been a tendency to overload the prospective helper with psychological theory at the expense of skills training. However, before proceeding to consider specific helping skills and training exercises, some guidelines and theoretical assumptions must be considered; indeed, 'there is nothing as practical as a good theory'.

The skills described in this chapter are biased towards a 'person-centred' and 'problem management' approach to counselling and as such are heavily influenced by the work of Carl Rogers and Gerard Egan. There are, of course, many theories of counselling and alternative approaches to helping. Frequently, counsellors use techniques and principles derived from different theories in an eclectic fashion. A thorough review of these different perspectives is provided by Nelson-Jones (1982).

Basic assumptions

The purpose of a 'client-centred' approach to counselling is to help the individual to help herself. Such an approach requires the 'client' to accept or 'own' her problem situation, to make a 'free choice' about solutions and to accept responsibility for the actions she takes to resolve her difficulties. The helper's responsibilities are to facilitate change by helping the client to explore her problems, to assist in identifying acceptable and workable solutions and to encourage the client to carry out whatever actions or solutions have been agreed. Helping, using this model, does not include:

1   *Telling the client what to do.* 'If I were you I'd go and see the Director of Nurse Education and complain about. . . . '
2   *Analysing and explaining the individual's difficulties.* 'Ah! Well you see your problem is that you've never cared for someone who is dying before and the reason you're feeling guilty is because. . . . '
3   *Applying your solution to their problem.* 'I know exactly how you feel. When I failed my final examinations, what I did was. . . . '
4   *Being judgemental.* 'Well that's a fine mess you've got yourself into. I can't imagine what you were thinking of. If you're expecting sympathy from me. . . . '

This last example illustrates one potentially major problem or obstacle in a helping relationship. In the Health Service there has been a tendency to use the term 'counselling' to describe a procedure used in the disciplinary process; this activity would be more accurately labelled as a 'disciplinary interview'. Further, there is the problem of role conflict. A student may have personal difficulties that are reflected in unacceptable professional behaviour. The ward sister may simultaneously, as manager, wish to discipline the student but also, as a helper, provide assistance. A student who has failed an assessment may seek help from his tutor but, in addition to 'counselling', the tutor may be obliged to 'warn the student formally' of the dismissal consequences of subsquent failure. These quite different roles are not mutually exclusive but they cannot be exercised simultaneously. Boundaries and terms of reference must be established so that both parties are quite clear about the objectives of their interaction. In many circumstances these dual roles can exist in parallel. However, *confidentiality* is fundamental to a helping relationship and information gained through the counselling relationship must not be used by the 'helper' when in a managerial role. There are no degrees of confidentiality — it is absolute. Confidentiality is a complex issue and these dilemmas cannot be resolved in one short chapter on counselling. Bryce Taylor (1983) makes two salutory observations:

'If you are genuine about making the client responsible for the content and disclosure in a session, then you must be prepared to take what comes.
  What goes on in a session is not your property, it is that of your client, and you are not at liberty to use it in any way without his or her knowledge or consent. You are not on a fact-finding mission for another agency.'

The helping relationship

A variety of characteristics are apparent in an effective helping relationship. Significant features of this helping climate are:

— The relationship is empathic; the helper understands the experiences and feelings of the client and this understanding is conveyed by the helper.
— The client and the helper relate well to each other.
— The helper is sensitive to the client's difficulties and sticks closely to his problems.
— The client feels able to say exactly what he likes.
— The relationship is based upon natural confidence and trust.

Rogers (1957) considers that three core conditions are necessary for the helper to be effective:

1 *Genuineness* is about being· authentic, being oneself and not employing facades. It requires openness, honesty and the use of appropriate self-disclosure. It means being spontaneous and not acting out some predetermined role or plan of action.
2 *Unconditional positive regard* means demonstrating respect and non-judgemental acceptance of the client's dilemma. It means valuing the individual's uniqueness and not applying conditions to acceptance. It is the ability to demonstrate to the client that he is worth while and has the capacity to overcome his current difficulties.
3 *Empathy*. There is no 'objective reality'; each of us perceives the world differently. Empathy means understanding the clients' experiences and feelings from *their* frame of reference and entering into their 'reality'. It means conveying to the client that he is understood. Huxley (1963) notes: 'To see ourselves as others see us is a most salutary gift. Hardly less important is the capacity to see others as they see themselves.'

Of these core conditions, Rogers considers empathy to be the central condition of the counselling relationship. Other observers describe collectively the three core conditions as 'basic empathy'. The evidence seems to suggest that these conditions are vital for a successful counselling relationship.

Self-awareness

The major resource that a helper brings to the counselling relationship is himself; consequently, the more complete his understanding of himself, the greater his capacity for self-awareness, the more effective he will be as a counsellor. Helpers need to have a positive and accepting view of themselves. The individual who is self-deprecating is unlikely to promote self-acceptance in his clients. A healthy self-concept, however, is not based on an assumption or illusion but on self-examination. Individuals who acceptingly acknowledge the discrepancy between their 'ideal self' and 'real self', the person they would wish to be and the person they are, are more likely to have a positive view of the worth and dignity of others. Self-awareness also implies being aware of the limits of one's knowledge and ability; this may be reflected by the individual actively studying, undertaking further training or seeking the assistance of a more experienced colleague. Of course, self-awareness is not a quality that is specific to counselling, it is a prerequisite for all dimension of helping. The view previously expressed in this book is that self-awareness is fundamental to the nursing role and, therefore, to nurse education. As such, experientially based self-awareness training should be predominantly positioned in nursing curricula. The range of experiences for self-awareness training is becoming increasingly extensive. *You and Me* (Egan 1977) is a particularly useful training manual and includes many individual and group exercises, as in the following examples.

Some questions about my interpersonal style (extract)   (© 1977 Wadsworth Inc., Brooks/Cole Publishing Co, Pacific Grove, California, USA) Ask yourself the following questions:

How much of my day is spent relating to people?

Do I have many friends or very few?

Is my life too crowded with people?

Do I plan to get together with others, or do I leave getting together to chance — if it happens, it happens?

Do I choose to be with people who will do what I want to do?

Do I feel that I need my friends more than they need me, or is it the opposite?

Do I take others for granted?

Do others see me as self-centred? If so, how?

Am I my real self when I'm with others, or do I play games and act phony at times?

Do I ever talk to others about the strengths and the weaknesses of our relationship?

Am I an active listener — that is, do I both listen carefully and then respond to what I've heard?

Do I enjoy it when others share with me whatever is important in their lives, including their secrets and their deepest feelings?

What people am I close to now?

Are there many different ways of being close to others? What are these ways? Which ways do I prefer?

Is it easy for others to know what I'm feeling?

Do I try to control others by my emotions — for instance, by being moody? Do I manipulate others?

Does feeling left out and lonely play much of a part in my life?

Can other people scare me easily?

Do I ignore or reject others who might want to get closer to me?

Do I like to control others, to get them to do things my way? Do I let others control me? Do I give in to others much of the time?

Am I willing to compromise — that is, to work out with another person what would be best for both of us?

Do I feel responsible for what happens in my relationships with others, or do I just let things 'take their course'?

At school or at work, do I treat people as people or do I see them as just other workers or just other students?

Am I willing to allow others to be themselves?

In what ways am I too cautious or too careful in relating to others? What are my fears?

Do I share my values with others?

Exercise 1   Which question did you find the most difficult to answer?
Which questions would you be afraid to discuss in your training group?

Exercise 2   Using the set of questions as a guide, write a short, one-page description of your present interpersonal style. On the one hand write only what you would be willing to read or show to your fellow group members; on the other hand, try to show a side of you that you think you do not usually let others see.

A model of helping

The model of helping proposed here is a 'problem management' or 'problem-solving' approach. In our everyday lives we use problem-solving sequences of the type illustrated in Fig. 7.1.

It is precisely the sequence applied to diagnosing and rectifying the problem with a car that will not start or to planning the annual summer holiday. It is also the approach advocated for the delivery of nursing care — where it is called the 'nursing process'. Frequently, this sequence of events is described as a 'cycle', which implies uninterrupted passage from one stage to the next. For ease of expression and understanding this is very convenient but it does conceal the dynamic relations of the various elements. The point here is that quite frequently problem-solving plans have to be changed because 'new' information becomes available or an intended course of action is no longer possible. Alternatively, what was previously considered to be a principal objective is eclipsed by another — consequently, each stage is in direct relationship with the others. In the next section of this chapter the skills of helping will be discussed under the headings of a problem-solving sequence but, in reality, the helper may well be using skills associated with different parts of the 'cycle' simultaneously.

Summary

In summarising this section on theory and principles of counselling and before

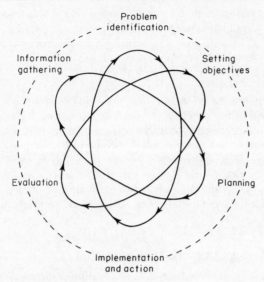

Fig. 7.1   Problem-solving sequence

proceeding to consider the practical skills required, it is worth reaffirming the purpose of the helping relationship. In his three-stage model of helping, Egan (1986) describes the following helping framework (Fig. 7.2):

Stage I   Clients' problem situations are explored and clarified. Clients cannot possibly manage problem situations unless they are understood — identification of the problem is described as *the current scenario*.

Stage II   Goals based on an understanding of the problem situation are set — *the preferred scenario*.

Stage III   Action — ways of accomplishing goals are devised, implemented and evaluated. These are the means of moving the client from her *current scenario* to her *preferred scenario*.

Counselling skills and practice

It is possibly self-evident that helping or counselling requires time, not necessarily a lot of time, but that time must be exclusively devoted to the client and be free of

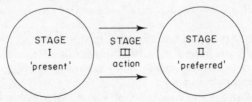

Fig. 7.2   Model of helping (Egan 1986)

interruptions and distractions. Frequently, ward offices are totally unsuited for this purpose. How much time depends on a number of variables but not least on how much time you can reasonably afford. A ward sister or a trained nurse is unlikely to be able to devote much more than thirty minutes on any single occasion to helping a student with a problem.

What is important here, is, that a boundary is set, so that the client knows exactly how much time there is at her disposal. Additionally, there must be clarity about the purpose of the meeting so that this cannot be misconstrued by the client. A 'person-centred' and 'problem solving' model assumes that the client, aided by the helper, will assume responsibility for the management of her problem; consequently, she needs to know how this can be achieved. The model does not belong to the helper and should not be concealed from the client. As a client group, student nurses can easily appreciate a brief explanation of the process — if they are to help themselves it will certainly aid if they know what is going on.

Information gathering and problem identification

If the helper is to empathise with the client's problem situation, she must listen attentively and, in turn, confirm with the client that she has understood what is being said. Active listening conveyed by the helper and experienced by the client is a prerequisite of effective helping. Active listening or attending is not as common as might be supposed. In theory a model of listening might be represented as shown in Fig. 7.3.

The process of listening to another person is often interfered with by our own thoughts, problems and feelings. When you are thinking about what you want to say it is difficult to attend to what is being said.

Basic attention

A fundamental requirement of the helper is to convey to the 'client' that she is being listened to. The experience of successful counsellors suggests that the following are useful sequences:

— Maintaining a comfortable distance, adopt a posture of relaxed alertness; face the client square on, leaning slightly forward; keep arms and legs unfolded.
— Maintain good eye contact, not a hard gaze but a soft, involved eye contact.
— Avoid extremes of movement such as fidgeting or sitting completely still.
— Avoid physical barriers such as a table or the arm or back of a chair.

Exercise In pairs, one partner is briefed to 'disclose' an issue that currently concerns her, but is advised that this should not be too serious a problem. Separately, the other partner is briefed initially to listen attentively to her partner's 'problem' but gradually to appear distracted and bored, to check her watch, occasionally look out of the window, and so on. After five minutes the interaction is stopped and the partners, in turn, discuss their experiences.

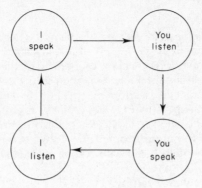

In reality the sequence is often:

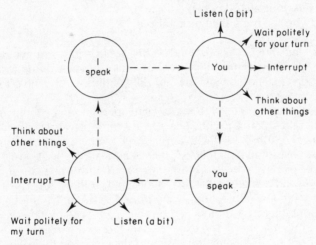

Fig. 7.3   Model of listening

Minimum encouragement and silence

There is evidence that inexperienced helpers are eager to respond to their clients, to the extent that they may interrupt before the other person has finished what she wanted to say. However, giving minimum encouragement by nodding, smiling, using sounds like 'Um-hmm' and 'Yeh' or comments as 'I see', 'Do go on', 'Yes' or simply repeating a word or two from the cient's last phrase has been demonstrated to increase substantially what the client has to say.

Exercise   In pairs, one partner is briefed to 'disclose' an issue of current concern to her, but is advised that this should not be too serious a problem. Separately, the other partner is briefed to use only minimal encouragement when listening to her partner. After five minutes the interaction is stopped and experiences are shared.

Questioning

In gathering information and identifying problems it is necessary for the helper to ask questions, particularly when the client finds it difficult to talk. However, a series of unrelenting questions may be experienced by the client as an interrogation. It is useful to distinguish between open and closed questions. Closed questions severely restrict the freedom to reply and tend to invite 'Yes' or 'No' or some factual information. This may be entirely appropriate at times, but a succession of closed questions is likely to accumulate information that is neither used or understood. In contrast, open questions encourage the client to talk freely: such questions often begin with 'What', 'How' and 'Could':

— 'What exactly do you mean by . . . ?'
— 'What do you think would happen if . . . ?'
— 'How do you feel when your patients . . . ?'
— 'How has your attitude changed since . . . ?'
— 'Could you tell me a little more about . . . ?'

'Why?' questions are frequently used — but are possibly best avoided. 'Why?' questions require an explanation and, as many people are unaware of their precise reasons for their behaviour, are difficult if not impossible to answer.

Exercise   For a group of eight to twelve participants, prepare three piles of plain cards, about sixteen cards in each pile. On the cards of two piles write at random either 'open' or 'closed'. On the third pile write a series of general topics such as 'Horseriding', 'My Summer Holiday', 'Nurse Education', 'Breakfast', and so on. Turn the three piles face down. One member of the group takes the top card from the topics pile and two others the top card from the other piles. The topic is read out and the members of the group are required to ask either an open or closed question about the topic as identified on their card. The process is repeated to involve all group members. The exercise concludes with members reflecting on the experience and discussing the ease and difficulty and the value and limitations of using open and closed questions.

Exercise   With a partner, conduct a 'helping' interview, experiment with a variety of questioning techniques and record your questions and answers in the following way:

Exact words used in the question	Outcomes in terms of length and quality of response	Is this an open or closed question

Reflection of content and feelings

One of the indications of empathy is the ability to feed back to the client what has been said and the accompanying feelings that the client is expressing. Reflecting is a method of demonstrating that you understand without judging or evaluating what has been expressed. Reflections enable the client to see herself more clearly and assist the helper in checking that she really does understand. It is not always easy to sort out the feelings from the content that is being expressed. Skilled helpers are able to do both simultaneously, although at times it may be more appropriate to focus on one rather than the other. From the point of view of training, it is useful to consider the skills of reflecting content and reflecting feelings separately.

Reflecting content (paraphrasing)

Paraphrasing is not merely repeating exactly what the client has said. It is the skill of putting the essential meaning of what has been said into other words. It might mean using a key word or phrase that seemed particularly important.

Client: 'Everything was going so well. I used to enjoy going out with my friends and really looked forward to work, but things are just falling apart. I've lost interest, I've no enthusiasm, I'm just low. I've been late on the ward twice recently and if I don't get down to some work I'm going to fail my exams, and that worries me a lot.'

Helper: 'So you've lost interest in things, it's affecting your work and you think you could fail your exams.'

When paraphrasing it is useful to be tentative, which could mean prefacing the reflection with 'What you seem to be saying is that . . . ' or concluding the reflection with ' . . . Is that it?' This not only encourages the client to carry on but conveys the concern that what is being said should be clearly and accurately understood. Individuals who are distressed and confused sometimes give rambling, even incoherent, accounts of their problems and it is difficult for the helper to understand what is really being said. A simple admission such as 'I really do want to understand but I'm not sure what you're saying', apart from encouraging the client to restate the problem, is an indication of honesty and conveys genuiness and concern. Clarifying is a powerful way of focusing on the significant issues. It helps to move the conversation forward and assists the client in identifying what she really wants to talk about. This is achieved through questioning, paraphrasing and reflecting feelings.

Exercise   In pairs, one partner talks, about an everyday problem. The other repeats exactly what is said — 'parrots'. Roles are reversed. Partners then discuss their experiences.

Exercise   In a group of six to ten, the facilitator invites one member of the group to discuss a real but not-too-serious problem. The other participants actively listen. The facilitator randomly selects one of the group to 'paraphrase' what has been said. The accuracy of the reflection is checked out with the 'client'. The participant who was paraphrasing then describes a problem, and so on.

Reflecting feelings

Reflecting feelings is different from reflection of content, the emphasis being on the overt or underlying feelings in what the client is saying. This skill of reflecting focuses upon the emotions and feelings of the client; inevitably, feelings play an important part in the problem that the client presents. This selective attention by the helper will encourage the other person to explore feelings rather than content. For example, using the previous illustration but this time focusing on feelings, the reflection might be:

Client: 'Everything was going so well . . . that worries me a lot.'
Helper: 'You're feeling down and when you think about your exams, that frightens you a lot.'

Again, it is useful to be tentative by prefacing the reflection with 'I sense you're feeling . . . ' or 'I imagine that you feel . . . '. The client may have mixed or even conflicting feelings: when these are reflected back this helps the individual to clarify what are the important issues. Sometimes there is a difference between the feeling stated and those expressed non-verbally. It can be useful to confront the client with this discrepancy:

'You say when you think about your exams it worries you a lot, yet as you talk about it you seem perfectly at ease.'

Exercise   Feelings or emotions can be difficult to label and describe. In pairs, firstly 'brainstorm' and list as many feeling words as you can. You will probably have words like:

Happy, sad, ashamed, bored, insecure, afraid, angry, hurt, loving, confused, rejected, trusting, free, guilty, satisfied, distressed, amused — and many more.

Using your list; incorporate each word into a sentence describing what was happening when you felt the emotion: 'I felt really happy when. . . . '

Exercise   Words are construed differently by different people — the same words have different meanings.
In pairs, brainstorm a list of feeling words (as above). Alternatively using each word, describe how you feel when you have this emotion: 'When I'm sad, I feel really down, I don't feel too good about myself. . . . '

Summarising

Summarising brings all the facets of the conversation together. It is a natural way of bringing a session to a close, or at the start of a session confirming in the minds of both participants what was said at a previous meeting. It is useful to encourage the client to summarise: 'So what do you think are the important things we've been talking about?' It also helps the client capture the essence of her difficulties and gives her a sense of movement towards solving whatever problem she has.

Problem identification

This first stage of the helping sequence has been concerned so far with developing a trusting relationship based on the helper's respect, genuineness and empathy with the client. The skills described have been concerned with understanding and appreciating the client's difficulties and enabling her to gain a greater understanding of her problem. The problem with problems is that they are frequently expressed in vague terms, but if specific action is to be taken the problem has to be stated specifically:

Vague: 'I've had enough.'
Specific: 'I find nursing elderly people very stressful.'

Further, problems rarely have clear and simple solutions; if they had, they would not be problems.

Problem: 'I started smoking six months into my training and can't give it up.'
Solution: 'Stop smoking!!'

Another problem with problems is that frequently there are secondary rewards in the behaviour that is considered to be a problem. The client needs to be helped to understand what these rewards are if she is to deal with her difficulties more effectively. At this stage the client may evade the problem or simply blame her dilemma on other people.

'Sister's always finding fault, it really screws me up, that's what makes me smoke.'

An appropriate and sensitive reflection will help the client to challenge the way she is managing her situation.

'So, it's Sister who makes you smoke?'

Challenging is a powerful technique for moving clients forward; however, if used to 'shock', if used insensitively and inappropriately, instead of helping the client, it will have negative and regressive consequences.

Finally, the client has to 'own' the problem — it is hers, and it is her responsibility. Of course, identifying and owning a problem does not actually change a thing. Not infrequently, counselling stops there because occasionally the client feels the consequences of change are worse than the current situation (scenario), but more frequently because the helper, having talked through the problem, leaves the client to 'get on with it'. Understanding the problem is essential but, on occasion, far too much time can be spent wandering around and around in stage I, repeatedly examining, refining and defining the problem.

> 'Assessment for the sake of Assessment, Exploration for the sake of Exploration, and Insight for the sake of Insight are all useless; they are successful to the degree that they enable the client to construct a more desirable scenario in terms of realistic goals or objectives' (Egan 1986).

Many students who seek or require assistance have thought deeply about their difficulties, have mentally rehearsed what they want to say, are intelligent and articulate. Consequently, problem identification might be achieved relatively quickly. The issue now is:

'If it wasn't this way — how would it be.'

Setting objectives and planning

Once the client understands her problem situation she may need assistance in identifying realistic objectives. Such objectives should reveal an awareness of the following:

1   Clients can be overwhelmed by the enormity of the task ahead. Objectives should be broken down into units that are workable and clients feel they can manage.
2   The individual needs to know clearly what the target is and whether it has been achieved. Objectives should be unambiguous and stated in a be-haviourally descriptive way, so that achievement is measurable.
3   The client owns the problem; she must also own the objective and therefore it must be acceptable to her if she is committed to attaining it.

Objectives should always be elicited from the client and not given by the helper. The counsellor can encourage the individual to brainstorm alternative objectives, although these may well be limited and painful choices will have to be made. The helper can assist here by encouraging the client to consider the consequences of her actions. Expedient short-term solutions may ultimately pose long-term complications and difficulties. Once all the potential objectives have been examined, the client needs to make a decision based on her own priorities. During this step the helper's role is to encourage the client to make a choice, and, once this is made, to help the client commit herself to it. One useful strategy for reinforcing the client's commitment is to examine the factors that will help her to reach her objective and those factors that might hinder her progress. Again, the client is encouraged to brainstorm, on this occasion, all those factors, direct and indirect, that will help to achieve the objective, and then the factors that hinder or restrain progress. It is useful if the client writes these down, not only so that factors are not forgotten but because seeing the problem, the objective and the factors that will help or hinder on paper can reassure the client that progress is being made (Fig. 7.4).

Problem: I haven't prepared for my examinations	
HELPING FACTORS	**HINDERING FACTORS**
1 I want to be a registered nurse.	1 I get bored easily.
2 Explain problem to boyfriend.	2 I like going out.
3 Get someone to help me with a study plan.	3 I'm tired when I finish on the ward.
4 Find some quiet place to work.	4 My boyfriend complains if we don't go out.
5 Making a contract with myself to study each day.	5 I don't know where to start.
6 Ask people to be quiet.	6 The nurses' home is too noisy.
7 Join a tutorial group.	7 My friends will think I'm a 'swat'.
8 Go out less often.	8 Nobody else seems to bother studying.
9 Go to bed early.	9 I'm not sure its worth all the effort.
10 Get my boyfriend to help me study.	
11 Keep a progress chart.	
12 I'll get a pay rise.	

Objective:
Within one week to have developed and commenced a scheme of study

Fig. 7.4   Table of helping and hindering factors

Of course, some of these factors are more important or more powerful than others and it might be useful for the client to underline those factors that will most strongly influence movement towards or away from the objective, as these will certainly influence her plan of action. The plan of action is concerned with *maximising* those factors that will help progress to the objectives and *minimising* or neutralising factors that will hinder. Whilst objectives describe the desired outcome, the plan identifies the step to be taken to achieve it. Using the previous example, the plan agreed by the client might be as shown in Fig. 7.5.

	ACTION	ACHIEVEMENT DATE
1	With personal tutor, undertake appraisal of areas of strength and weakness.	Day 2
2	Prepare study scheme based on above appraisal: two hours each day.	Day 3
3	Go out three times a week and relax — a reward for keeping up with (2) above.	Day 7 or sooner
4	Discuss with boyfriend — ask for help with revision — be assertive.	Day 4
5	Ask neighbours to respect my right to reasonable peace and quiet.	Day 5
6	Keep a visual progress chart so I know what I've achieved.	Now

Fig. 7.5   Action plan

As the plan has been discussed from helping and hindering factors, it could be a list of 'dos' and 'don'ts'. It is useful if a plan is stated in positive action terms — doing.

It is not necessary for the client to express formally her plan as illustrated above, although when this is done it has a contractual quality — the client contracting with herself to take specific actions by a predetermined date, the helper acting as a 'witness'. This reinforces the commitment to achieve the specific goals in an agreed time.

Exercise In pairs, using the following 'problems':

I am overweight.
I smoke.
I can't seem to relax.
I don't have enough time for my family.
I am always in debt.
. . . and others you might think of.

Brainstorm as many objectives as you can for each problem – let your imagination run free — be creative.

Implementation and evaluation

The client now has an understanding of her problem, has declared objectives for change and devised a plan that will achieve the objectives. Although much progress has been made by this stage, unless the plan is implemented the client's difficulties remain unresolved. The role of the helper at this stage is to encourage and support the client to take the planned course of action. Such action often means applying new or unused behaviours; permanent or relative changes in behaviour are called learning. Consequently, at this stage the helper can usefully apply learning principles — these were discussed in Chapter 2. However, it is useful to reiterate the motivating power of 'knowledge of results' and 'positive reinforcement'. At times it is not easy, from the client's perspective, to see exactly what progress is being made. The helper may assist by providing evidence of achievement: reward or 'positive reinforcement' are fundamental to behavioural change. The client needs to build rewards for success into her plan and the helper, through approval and encouragement, can provide reinforcement and assist in shaping the desired behaviour.

Role-modelling

A helper cannot be all things to all men (or women). However, through her interaction with her client she can demonstrate (model) useful interpersonal behaviour. Earlier in this chapter it was suggested that helpers should be 'self-aware'. A component of self-awareness is being assertive in relationships. This needs to be distinguished from other styles of behaviour.

Aggressive:	forcing people, attacking, intimidating, blaming, giving orders, dominating, violating the rights of others
Manipulative:	deceiving others, insincerity, being two-faced, using people, making others feel guilty
Submissiveness:	putting yourself down, not saying what you want, giving in, giving up responsibility: violating own rights
Assertive:	being honest in relationships, respect for self and others, making own decisions; accepting praise and criticism, neither violating own or other's rights

The helper in this model needs to be assertive in implementing her plans: so do clients. There is evidence that student nurses are encouraged to be submissive (Briggs 1986). Indeed, some of their difficulties may be directly associated with being insufficiently assertive, allowing themselves to be dominated and manipulated. The client may vicariously learn useful styles of assertion through the behaviour of her helper.

Role rehearsal

It is helpful if the plan is viewed optimistically but realistically: the helper can encourage the client to anticipate snags and obstacles. It can be useful if the helper and the student explore these, possibly by role-playing the potential difficulties. For example, using the earlier illustration the student may rehearse responding to a phone call when her boyfriend attempts to coerce or manipulate her into abandoning her planned evening of study, so that they can go out for a drink.

Finally, the effectiveness of the planned actions needs to be evaluated; the helper, with the client, can identify intended and unintended outcomes. If the client has failed to achieve her goal it may be because circumstances have changed and the plan would require amendment to take account of this. Action might not have been taken because the plan was unrealistic or because the client has avoided taking the agreed action. In this situation the helper, whilst being supportive and acknowledging the achievements that have been made, can sensitively challenge the client. Of evaluation, Connor et al (1984) suggest that the skills in this situation are being able to summarise and maybe challenge in a tentative way. Positive reinforcement should always be given at this stage, even in the face of apparent failure. The client should be rewarded for coming back to keep her appointment! New shaping strategies may then be worked out to help the client achieve the new objective and regain momentum.

Helpers can experience some difficulty in terminating a session, or the helping relationship itself. In some respects this is even more difficult for the ward sister 'doing counselling' than the 'professional counsellor', not because of different skills levels but because of her day-to-day working contact with the client. The problem here is essentially one of managing boundaries: this includes boundaries of space (where we meet), boundaries of time (for how long we meet) and boundaries of role (why we meet). Some initial suggestions have already been made about the first two boundaries. Sometimes the relationship is terminated because the client does not keep her appointment. How ever impolite or insensitive this may seem, it is the individual's right to terminate the helping relationship. If it is evident at the first meeting that it will be helpful to meet on future occasions then a boundary can be set. 'Shall we meet for half an hour once a week for the next three weeks?' This usefully identifies a potential point for termination. The boundary can always be adjusted in the light of experience, although it is unlikely that a trained nurse would be able to enter into a long-term 'counselling relationship' with a student. However, relatively short-lived helping relationships are difficult to terminate, but if they are not, this has the potential to create role confusion for future work encounters between the trained nurse and the student. Endings are never entirely satisfactory and 'goodbyes' are very difficult, but when the problem-solving work is done it needs to be acknowledged. At the final meeting it is useful to discuss openly feelings about termination before formally parting and reverting to respective working roles.

Exercise   In threes (trios). This training exercise can be used to practise one specific skill or a series of skills. The three participants adopt the role of (1) client, (2) helper, (3) observer. These roles require:

— The '*client*' to present, preferably, a 'real' problem that is not too serious which she feels confident in disclosing to the trio

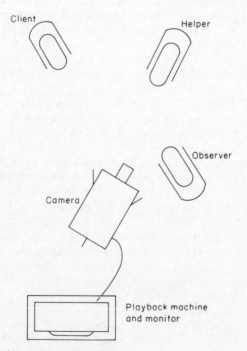

Fig. 7.6   Layout for videotaping an exercise

SELF-ASSESSMENT

This rating scale is designed to assist you identify the 'micro' skills of the counselling process with which you feel confident and those that may requre further skills development.

		Strongly Agree				Strongly Disagree
1	I am the type of person that people approach when in 'trouble'.	I...........I...........I...........I...........I
2	When 'counselling' I always ensure 'boundaries' of time and space.	I...........I...........I...........I...........I
3	I listen actively to what people say.	I...........I...........I...........I...........I
4	My 'non-verbal' style conveys active attention and concern to the 'client'.	I...........I...........I...........I...........I
5	I am able accurately to reflect what the client has said without changing the esential meaning.	I...........I...........I...........I...........I
6	I can construct open questions that move the conversation forward.	I...........I...........I...........I...........I
7	I can use silence effectively in the helping process.	I...........I...........I...........I...........I
8	I am able to detect and label clients feelings accurately.	I...........I...........I...........I...........I
9	Despite my own values I am non-judgemental of 'clients' views and behaviours.	I...........I...........I...........I...........I
10	I can helpfully summarise what the 'client' has said.	I...........I...........I...........I...........I
11	I am prepared to disclose things about myself if necessary.	I...........I...........I...........I...........I
12	I am able to disassociate my role of 'manager' from that of helper.	I...........I...........I...........I...........I
13	I am able to end a counselling session/the helping contract in a positive way.	I...........I...........I...........I...........I

Fig. 7.7   Counselling skills — a rating scale

— the 'helper' to practise and demonstrate a skill such as 'reflecting feelings' using the client's material
— the 'observer' unobtrusively and actively to observe the interaction between the helper and the client

The client–helper interaction lasts 15 minutes and is then stopped by the observer. The observer then gives feedback to the helper. This should be based on what happened, on specific observed behaviours and should encourage self-assessment by the helper. The observer's role is not to give advice or to suggest how they should have done it. Feedback should last for five minutes. Each participant then changes roles. This exercise can also be augmented by the use of video so that participants can collectively or individually review the interactions (see Fig. 7.6).

Skills training

In this chapter an attempt has been made not so much to discuss the theory of counselling but to describe the practical skills that can be employed in helping. Some suggestions for skills development exercises have also been made. Like other skills, 'counselling' can be improved by practice and by helpful feedback on performance. Egan (1986) suggests the following steps in a training programme:

1 Cognitive understanding — through reading and lectures, clarified by discussion and questions.
2 Behavioural clarity — through observing the skills, this may be done 'live' or with film or video.
3 Skills practice — trainees practise skills with one another and receive feedback from the trainer and one another.
4 Maintenance — trainees reflect on the training process itself. Steps 1 to 3 deal with the task of training. Step 4 is concerned with seeing to the feelings and individual needs of the trainees.

A major contribution in this area is the skills training programme developed by Connor *et al* (1984) *Listening and Responding*. This package is designed specifically for nurses and conforms closely to the steps described above.

In concluding this chapter on counselling skills, the reader is invited to assess her own skills using the rating scale shown in Fig. 7.7.

References

Briggs A (1972) *Report of the Committee on Nursing (Briggs Report)*. London: H M S O
Briggs K (1986) Speak your mind. *Nursing Times–Mirror*, **82**(26)
Connor M et al (1984) *Listening and Responding: Communication Skills in Nursing Care*. St John: The College of Ripon and York
Egan G (1977) *You and Me*. Monterey: Brooks-Cole
Egan G (1986) *The Skilled Helper*. Monterey: Brooks-Cole
Huxley A (1963) *The Doors of Perception*. New York: Harper & Row
Nelson-Jones R (1982) *The Theory and Practice of Counselling Psychology*. Eastbourne: Holt, Rhinehart & Winston
Nicklin P J (1987) Violence to the Spirit. *Senior Nurse* **6**(5) 10–12
Rogers C R (1957) The necessary and sufficient conditions of therapeutic personality change. *Journal of Consulting Psychology*, **21**
Taylor B (1983) *Working with Others: Aspects of Helping and Counselling*. York: Oasis Publications
United Kingdom Central Council (1984) *Code of Professional Conduct*, para 11. London: U K C C
Watts A G (ed) (1977) *Counselling at Work*. London: S C A C, Bedford Square Press

8
Recording and Reporting

The chapter on the principles of assessment (Chapter 4) has dealt with the documentation and recording of assessment outcomes. Similarly, the chapter on evaluation (Chapter 9) will provide examples of methods of recording data to be used for appraising and evaluating parts of a course and, indeed, whole courses. Reporting is equally a feature of both the assessment and evaluation components of the curriculum process and is therefore incorporated into the respective chapters. What does require commenting upon is the daily task of keeping appropriate records by both the student and the supervisor, together with the preparation of reports and their giving or receiving.

The nature and purpose of record-keeping

For the student nurse the significance of keeping records is to help with the learning process either as something to refer back to, i.e. an *aide memoir*, or as a relevant piece of information in a series, e.g. a measurement or value to be used for comparison purposes. In the first example, a student may participate in a particular learning experience and acquire some useful information such as observing a particular syndrome or unusual presentation of symptoms. Although important at the time, it is likely that the student may not need to refer to that experience until some later date — hence the significance of accurately recording the details. This is even more relevant if the information has to be passed on to other people.

The second use of record-keeping may be illustrated by the student who is interested in being able to compare such things as performance, knowledge, or feelings as she progresses through a course or course unit. It may be that she has been present when a patient has died. Knowing that this is not an uncommon occurrence in some areas of care provision, the student may wish to keep a record of her thoughts and feelings that surrounded the occasion. Subsequently when a similar situation is experienced, it may be helpful to the student again to record the associated emotions and compare them with earlier experiences. Many students may keep copious records of their daily activities in both practical settings and study periods. This will prove to be beneficial only if the detail recorded is significant and related to the learning objectives being achieved. Recording irrelevant data is not only a waste of time but can disguise or detract from the important facts that should be understood and retained. The role of the nurse who is supervising the student must be not only to give sound guidance on what the student should record for learning purposes but also to check the material recorded at frequent periods during the unit of experience. Another important aspect of written records is that of confidentiality. The qualified nurse must at all times impress upon the student the importance of using recorded information about patients only for her own educational purposes and not to divulge any part of such information and, indeed, not to leave the records unattended where they may either be lost or be seen by unauthorised people.

A further reason why the student may wish, or be asked, to keep records is if she is to contribute to either the evaluation of that part of the course or a review of the ward or department as an effective care environment.

Record-keeping and the supervisor

Supervisors of students, whether they be ward sisters, community nurses, staff nurses or midwives, will no doubt keep records of individual students to whom they act as mentors. Additionally, the supervisor may keep records of the experiences received by the students so that each can be judged as to its value in providing sound learning opportunities and reinforcers of good practice.

The relevance of maintaining continuous records of a student's performance becomes obvious when at the end of an allocation period the supervisor has to make written statements about the student or award a score or grade to aspects of performance. In the absence of regular records of student progression it is all too easy to recall either the instances of weak knowledge, mistakes in carrying out a nursing procedure, or a faulty attitude, and pay undue emphasis to them when in reality they were the exception rather than the rule. That is not to ignore their significance: the supervisor must sharply draw them to the student's attention. However, they can be seen out of overall context and detract from the strengths displayed by the student. The reverse of this is equally important and the rare moment of brilliance in a student's performance must not be allowed to overshadow an otherwise unsafe and unsatisfactory progress. Accurate records frequently kept will be invaluable when arriving at an end-of-unit appraisal. Records on their own or taken out of context can be misleading or meaningless, but used in conjunction with other information may reveal strengths and weaknesses or assist in problem identification. If the supervisor maintains a record of the student's pattern of timekeeping, what might this reveal over a period of, say, two to three months? Repeated late arrivals for early duties may be due to no more than late nights and an inability to rise early. Linked with lateness for afternoon duties, 'pinching' the extra ten minutes at meal breaks, eagerness to go off duty early and the ocassional day's 'ringing in' sick with migraine or tummy upset reveal a more serious problem. It is very rare in this type of behaviour pattern to see a high level of performance and learning achievement within the student's progress. Mediocre standards of care, apathy towards learning and unacceptable attitudes to peers and supervisors are more readily observed.

Having put all these symptoms together by using accurate records it remains for the supervisor in conjunction with the personal tutor to make a diagnosis. There is usually an identifiable cause. The root of the problem may lie outside the work situation. One director of nurse education reports a few occurrences recently of the boyfriends of student nurses taking exception to their girls caring for male patients, so much so in one instance that the student dare not talk about work in her boyfriend's presence. Whilst seeming almost ridiculous to a third person, trouble with boyfriends is just one example of the very real pressures students may experience away from the work situation. At work, there are equally as many hidden pressures and anxieties facing the student, and some of these anxieties that affect learning progress have been described by Birch (1983).

Record-keeping and the nurse teacher

Most nurse teachers, if they are involved in a system that offers every student a personal tutor facility, will have interest in and responsibility for twenty or more students at any one time. The nurse supervisor in the mentor role will only have one or maybe two students whilst the student herself has only herself to worry about. It is likely that the nurse teacher will act as personal tutor to each student for the whole length of the course. Comprehensive record-keeping can help the teacher to maintain an accurate profile on each student with a better chance of anticipating problems and applying corrective treatments if the profile begins to show an abnormal pattern. Approaching the end of the course the student will probably be applying for a staff nurse post within the same health authority or elsewhere. In either case it is likely to be the personal tutor, in conjunction with the course tutor, who will be asked to supply a reference in support of the student's application. Whilst formal records of the student's progress will be referred to, it is often the information of a less formal type available from the personal tutor that is of equal significance. The tutor who keeps records of this type can often provide information about a student which may be of use in a wide range of circumstances other than providing references for future appointments. Occupational health matters, disciplinary situations, selection for special awards, membership of committees, working groups and curriculum teams are all realistic examples of how recorded information about students can be put to practical use.

Reference has already been made to the other role of nurse teachers, that of course tutor, where the teacher acts as the visible head of the course and ensures its smooth running by coordinating all of its component parts. Record-keeping other than the statutory and formal records of the course and its students may again be of real value. A weekly or even daily jotting down of any significant occurrences, good experiences, bad moments, disasters or the like can assist the course tutor with periodic review and evaluation of course units by augmenting or assisting in the completion of formal evaluation documentation. At a less formal level, the course teacher can refer to his records when selecting 'horses for courses' — which student to participate in which particular learning environment. Matching personalities, optimising learning opportunities, creating maximum cooperation between students, facilitating good group dynamics — all are made that much easier through the use of good information. Record-keeping need not be the sole property of the allocations officers, clerical staff or managers; the nurse teacher can use it to great effect.

Methods of recording information

Diaries, journals, logs

Keeping records by using diaries is probably the most frequent system of recording information and to many people is synonymous with the keeping of a log. Often used on a daily basis, it is a method that requires a certain amount of self-discipline until it becomes a habit or part of one's daily routine. The journal approach is slightly different to the diary or log in that it tends to be written less frequently, e.g. weekly, and may take the form of narrative, whereas the log is more a short note or comment. All these systems of record-keeping can be adopted easily without the use of specific documentation or stationery. For the student, a simple daily note of a significant learning event, a valuable experience, a piece of new information or carrying out a new skill might be all that is necessary. The nurse supervisor would likewise record a good learning opportunity provided, the result of a specific patient-centred teaching activity and such things as the student's declared and observed needs and expectations that day. Nurse teachers are not always good at putting into practice what they preach. Having advocated the keeping of a diary or journal to the students and qualified nurses they may then omit to develop the practice themselves, not out of neglect or laziness but because they believe they can readily act upon or recall, when necessary, that which ought to be recorded. The teaching session that was a great success, a student-directed debate that was a total flop and the group discussion that got out of control: each of these situations, should they have happened to a teacher, would probably be remembered at some future date and avoided or modified if necessary. Recording a brief note at the time each happened is perhaps more than just keeping a record — it affords the teacher a second opportunity to think about the situation and its circumstances. This is equally applicable for the student and the qualified nurse.

Criteria sheets and grids

Keeping diaries and journals consists, in the main, of writing notes or comments on blank sheets of paper or the blank pages of a book. Completing criteria sheets or filling in grids sounds more structured or mechanistic, and developing these methods of record-keeping is partly the domain of appraisal and evaluation systems. Additionally, the teacher or nurse supervisor may use criteria sheets and grids with students who are undertaking learning assignments or participating in particular experiences, i.e. spending a week in local industry or carrying out a community-based project. The criteria sheet will guide the student to the type and amount of information required, together with the boundaries or parameters within which each must operate (Fig. 8.1). The grid will be used by the student to record the data collected and will also facilitate the presentation of the project findings.

Computers

An increasing number of hospitals, clinics and health centres are using computers at patient level. One common use of this form of technology is to record patient data in terms of nursing dependency from which workload indices can be calculated. The workload index will then dictate the nursing manpower required to provide the care to meet the dependency needs of the patient. It is a system for storing, retrieving and purposefully using information extracted from records. Those who are advocates of the patient-centred approach to nursing care might assert that the use of computers at patient level is impersonalising care. The opposite may be argued: because the dependency level of each patient features on the computer screen and the student can read the grades, add to them or change them, she thinks of each patient as having very real needs which require a specific amount of her time. By carrying out appropriate care the student can influence the level of dependency and adjust the data in the computer accordingly. The student is keeping a record and using the record-keeping facility of the computer to learn more about patient care.

The nature and purpose of reporting

Accuracy of reporting

Accurate reporting of factual material and events is not a strong characteristic of most people. When asked to describe in detail the series of events at, say, a motor car accident, most people will report less than half the facts accurately (this has often been verified on television in simulated accident settings). At the nurse/patient level can a student transmit accurately that information which is gained by observing a patient's condition or after talking with a patient? A student nurse may report to the ward sister that a particular patient has a chest pain. Apart from the anatomical location this report tells little — there is insufficient information for it to be of any use. More needs to be ascertained of both the quantity or severity of the pain and the quality or subjective description of it by the patient. Very often, the description by a student of something like a pain is distorted by her own perception, experience and threshold of pain. This illustration is given solely to emphasise that reporting must be accurate if it is to be useful. The ward sister who reports to the student's personal tutor that the student is late on duty every other day when in fact lateness has only occurred three times in the space of a month is perhaps unintentionally presenting an inaccurate account. It is an exaggeration and, in some cases, reflects the subjective feelings of the ward sister towards the student.

Objectivity and subjectivity of reporting

Reports are usually prepared and delivered for quite specific purposes, such as passing on information, giving advice and making judgements. A report will achieve a higher degree of objectivity if the person compiling it can focus precisely upon the topic of the report and not be side-tracked into other areas. If a nurse supervisor/mentor is to report to the personal tutor or to the student nurse

THE WORKING ENVIRONMENT

Students will spend a week in a working environment — a factory, a supermarket or an industrial plant — during which time they will be observing the environment and the work processes and eliciting answers to questions prepared in advance.

It has been established with employers that the students will be able to ask pertinent questions both of management and the workforce. In some cases the employers have asked to extend the questionnaire in order to improve health problems and increase standards of safety.

AIMS

For students to:

1   Discover the significance of occupational factors in the determination of health and disease

2   To help the process of achieving insight into the working lives of patients, in order to enhance communication through increased empathy

OBJECTIVES

At the end of the project the students should have begun to:

1   Understand some of the more important effects that occupational factors have in the determination of health and disease

2   Become aware of the working environment of the patient, in order to give appropriate advice

3   To have enhanced empathy with patients

CRITERIA

To be adapted for a particular place of work.

Type of industry
Number of employees
Different types of work

Different pay structures
Different sickness rules — re time allowed with pay
Different methods of reporting sick
Different methods of reporting for work

Overtime
Shift-work
Social structures of workforce

Is there an industrial nurse?
What is her role?

First aid attendant

Role of management
Industrial Relations Officer
Personnel Officer
Health and Safety Officer
Others

Special problems as seen by management

Special problems as seen by other groups of workers, i.e. office staff, shop floor

Canteen facilities, if any

Protective clothing
Who provides such clothing?
Do the workforce wear their protective clothing?
If not, why not?

Factors indicated by management that may inhibit health
Factors as seen by the workforce that may inhibit health
Other factors observed by you

Comments on social interactions as seen by you

1   Where did I go?

2   What did I go for?

3   What did I expect?

4   What did I find?

5   What did I conclude?

Use the questionnaire as a guide. You may have to adjust the questionnaire. Keep notes and write them up at the end of each day.

Produce a summary of your project and have a copy for the members of your group. You will be required to lead a seminar discussion on your project.

This discussion should last about 20–30 minutes. Try to involve all the members of the group. Draw the discussion to a close.

Fig. 8.1   An example of a criteria sheet

on the progress made in achieving a nursing competency then that, and that only, must be the focus of the report. It is of no consequence that the student is known to prefer another nursing specialty than the one currently being experienced. Any feeling the supervisor may have about the student's political or religious opinions must be ignored when presenting an objective analysis of nursing skills acquired by the student. Dilemmas of this nature are described by Dunn (1984) who feels that report preparation and giving requires very careful planning and thought on the part of the giver. What is required by the student is an educational comment and not a personal view. While supervisors of students acknowledge that reporting is a vital activity in the overall measurement of progress, Long (1976) points out that they also recognise that their assessment of students are often influenced by factors other than ability alone. Some felt that they were subjectively influenced by particular incidents, others by personality clashes and a very large number accepted that standards used by supervisors varied immensely. In the same piece of research, Long finds that half the ward sisters in the survey spent fewer than ten minutes on the preliminary interview with students. At the end of a student nurse's period of practical experience, two-thirds of the ward sisters spent fewer than thirty minutes in preparing the report *and* carrying out the final interview. Clearly, there is a wide variance in the degree of objectivity and diligence attached to the preparation and delivery of reports.

Reporting on student nurses

The chapters on principles of assessment and evaluation deal with the formal aspects of documenting progress and outcomes of student performance, together with the achievements of the course as a whole. What may require a little elaboration is the process of preparing reports and giving those reports to students as part of the curriculum activity. Quite often, the student may not acknowledge the report-receiving exercise as part of the educational process; it is sometimes perceived as some form of discipline or counselling activity which is unrelated to teaching or learning. This misconception may not be all that strange if the reporting session consists of no more than the one-way passage of information or criticism from 'above' to 'below'. For reporting to be an educational activity it needs to be staged carefully, with both parties being adequately prepared and the 'agenda' of items fully understood by the recipient. To introduce unexpected or unnecessary topics into the reporting session is both unfair and negative in educational terms. Similarly, for the student to adopt an uninterested and unresponsive approach as the recipient of a report is not an acceptable response to what should be a rewarding and stimulating interaction for both parties.

Not all reports can be delivered personally to the student. When this is the case, the report-giver should endeavour to meet the student at the next available opportunity or at least invite her to respond in writing to the points made in the report. What are the circumstances in which a nurse supervisor or a nurse teacher may need to produce a report on the student other than a formal progress assessment or practice-based test/examination? The following are offered as examples:

— Statement relating to practice-based objectives
— Fact-finding report following a complaint against the student
— Independent report in a discontinuation of training situation
— Report to the course tutor on a 'borderline' student
— Course tutor's report on progress within a course unit
— Course tutor/personal tutor's statement on a disciplinary issue facing the student
— Informal report on a piece of work completed and a good standard achieved

Reporting is frequently linked with passing judgements, making comments and levelling criticism. Accepting that these are necessary, the teacher and supervisor might consider also preparing a report when praise and reward is merited. A student may have had a piece of written work published; discharged patients may write to the ward sister praising the care received from a particular student; the ward sister may feel that as a student has contributed significantly to the effective running of the ward or department she wishes to say thank you and well done! A report that acknowledges and reflects praise is just as much part of the student's training file as a marked examination paper or a study block test score.

Introducing students to the skill of preparing written and oral reports should be done very early in the course — some would say from the first day, particularly if the course employs experiential approaches to teaching and learning. Exposing students to learning situations that require some form of reporting back, whether it is by the individual or as a group, is not difficult to engineer. Reinforcing successful reporting will give the student confidence in the future creation of written reports, each subsequent one becoming more proficient. Through identifying with the need for preparing reports and refining the skill to a high level the student will have attained a valuable communication tool. Although it can be practical within the assigned work of study periods its real value will be seen at the practical level, where accurate and objective reporting may influence the type of care the patient receives. The nurse supervisor must ensure that the student practises frequently.

Receiving reports

Far from being a passive activity, the receiving of written or verbal reports requires a high level of skill. If a student or any member of the care team has become proficient at preparing and delivering reports then unless these are acted upon in some way the reporter will quickly become apathetic to the whole process of keeping records and passing on information. The role of the recipient is to interpret or analyse the report and plan or implement a response with or without the assistance of the person who compiled the information.

Following a meeting of the students' representative committee, its chairman may have prepared a report about the unsatisfactory arrangements for students gaining community experience. How should the course tutor receive such a report and what may be the appropriate responses? Receipt of the report ought immediately to be acknowledged by the teacher together with an indication of how soon a response to the report can be expected. This procedure should be carried out by the teacher in a calm and professional manner, despite any potential for irritation or annoyance. When a detailed reply to the students' reports has been prepared the teacher may wish to attend the students' representative committee in order to present it live and answer any further questions that may arise. Such an approach is both purposeful and professional, showing that students' feelings and opinions are not only respected but taken seriously.

Where reports are received with bad grace and treated in a contemptuous manner the result is almost certain to be a total breakdown in effective communication, with the student being the loser, irrespective of who was to blame. Students are frequently asked to report upon the practical experience they have received on a ward or department. If a report is less than complimentary about one of the wards and its staff, how may the ward sister receive such a report? Again, the report should be received with good grace and treated seriously. It may be that it is an isolated critical report that is unsupported by other students who have been on the ward. If this is the case then it should be noted and replied to in a courteous and objective way, with copies to the personal tutor and course tutor. Where subsequent unfavourable reports are received from later student attendances, the ward manager must then begin to carry out in-depth investigations and problem identification.

Using recording and reporting to produce student profiles

Despite the wide range of measuring devices used to assess the level of attainment of the student and the degree to which competency is being achieved, there is still much about the student that either remains undiscovered or goes unrecorded. In practice, when a learning objective has been achieved it is ticked off a list: the score from a written examination is recorded on the student's card. Little is known about how the student felt when attempting to achieve the objective or what personal motivation led to reaching a high score in an examination. Progress reports completed by the student's supervisor following a period of practical experience tend to focus on what has been achieved or not achieved; very rarely is there comment on why and how goals were reached. Schools and colleges tend to use measuring devices that are determined by the subjects on the curriculum, argues Law (1984), which unfortunately do not help teachers to know more about their students as individuals. Some of the recording and reporting systems described earlier in this chapter will undoubtedly collect and transmit substantial amounts of information about individual students, but much of this data will be discarded or ignored mainly because it does not fit neatly into any recordable category in the student's documentation. A wealth of significant material is being lost which could not only help the teacher and practical supervisor to better understand the student but also play a key role in curriculum development and evaluation. No particular attention is paid to the expressed preferences of students in terms of nursing experiences when options may be available. If a student has a particular aptitude for caring for the elderly or handicapped, will this show as a positive feature in the student's records? When planning a particular student's allocation programme to a whole series of clinical experiences, does it matter if this does not take into account the individual's physical characteristics and skills, intellectual ability, social and cultural traits and personal interests? Perhaps a far more meaningful practical programme could be prescribed if some of these aspects of the student's make-up were considered. Creating profiles for each student need not be a complex matter: basic criteria which can form the main categories for record-keeping need to be agreed. These will include some of the following:

— Motivational needs	What works best for the student?
— Achievement expectations	Are these realistic?
— Hopes and aspirations	Can these be attained?
— Assumed skills	Are these confirmed?
— Strengths	Have these been demonstrated?
— Weaknesses	
— Aptitudes	Can these be exploited?
— Personality traits	Are these significant?
— Physical attributes	Do they have any relevance?
— Apprehensions	Real or imagined?

The above are just a few examples of the types of information that often come to light through the normal process of keeping records. If a base-line profile can be established at the commencement of a course and then be reviewed at appropriate intervals during that course, the resultant changes in the shape of the profile, considered alongside the formal assessment procedures and outcomes, should provide a more comprehensive and accurate account of the student's progress.

Can quality be recorded?

Quality in this context relates to the progress of the student in educational and performance terms. Recording quantitative attainment is not difficult to carry out: scores, grades, numbers of objectives achieved, ratios, percentages and averages are commonly used devices for recording quantitative data. How, then, or in what precise terms, can quality of progress or attainment be recorded and reported upon?

A King's Fund Project Paper on quality assurance suggests that to define the term quality it is necessary to refer to a number of other elements (Shaw 1986). These qualifying elements are given as 'appropriateness', 'equity', 'accessibility', 'effectiveness', 'acceptability' and 'efficiency'. Whilst quality as described by these elements is used to record patient care, it can be argued that the similarity with the provision of education or training is close. Of these proposed elements, which contribute to that which is called 'quality', Shaw claims the key element to be 'appropriateness'. Consider the following situation. The nurse supervisor or teacher gives the student a project or assignment as part of the learning programme. During the following days the student prepares the necessary information and plans how it should be presented, then compiles the project material and, finally, presents it to the supervisor as a completed assignment. The supervisor, on reading the student's presentation, quickly recognises that the student has misinterpreted or not properly understood the brief and has produced a totally futile piece of work that is not appropriate to the expectation of the assignment. Even though the student may have used sound educational principles and reputable research methodology, the outcome cannot be described as having quality because it is inappropriate to the requirements or expectations. When described like this, 'quality' would seem to be easier to record and report upon than quantitative attainment. With the emphasis in nursing education moving from summative measures to the more process-oriented formative approach, the need to develop systems for recording quality of attainment will increase. Which is more important to a student, to be told that the knowledge used in describing an aspect of patient care is very appropriate or that it would have earned 8 marks out of 10 in a test paper?

References

Birch J A (1983) Anxiety and conflict in nurse education. In Davis B (ed) *Research into Nurse Education*. London: Croom-Helm
Dunn D (1984) Have you done my report please, Sister? *Nursing Times*, **4**(2)
Law B (1984) *Uses and Abuses of Profiling*. New York: Harper & Row
Long P (1976) *International Journal of Nursing Studies*, **13**(2)
Shaw C D (1986) *Introducing Quality Assurance*, Project paper. London: King's Fund

9
The Nature and Purpose of Evaluation

Evaluation is arguably the least understood and most neglected element of curriculum design and development. Teachers often spend many hours carefully considering course aims, objectives, teaching and learning strategies. At planning team meetings detailed accounts of content matter, methods of presentation and analysis of resources will be examined. Once these very important issues have been resolved it is then, and only then, that the planning team will address the topic of course evaluation. All too frequently, evaluation can be identified as the afterthought attached to the rest of the curriculum strategy – an optional extra. Perhaps the reader may detect a note of cynicism but Lawton (1981) suggests that such an attitude is not unreasonable because it is a fact that issues of evaluation present some of the most difficult problems for curriculum planners.

The term 'evaluation' is not difficult to define when the prefix 'course' is used. This clearly discriminates it from anything to do with student assessment, which is sometimes, perhaps carelessly, called evaluation. Although terms such as 'the value of' and 'worth while' immediately come to mind, they need qualifying. Together with an indication of the effectiveness of a course one must consider its justification and consequences. A course may be very effectively conducted in both its content and teaching but it may no longer meet the needs for which it was designed: those needs may have changed. Courses in the field of mental illness and mental handicap provide typical examples of this. The course may produce a very competent and efficient nurse able to give care in the institutional setting of a large psychiatric hospital. An evaluation of the course would prove it to be totally effective. Fortunately, the provision of psychiatric care now has its focus within the community and the newly qualified nurse is ill-prepared to function in this changing environment. A new and radically different course is required.

Classification of evaluation models

The past twenty years have brought major changes in the field of general

124

education, in most cases backed by government money. During periods of financial restraint, concepts of accountability, cost-effectiveness and value for money emerge as key factors in the development of educational strategies. As questions relating to student attainment and teacher competency are raised it becomes increasingly necessary to measure accurately the outcomes of educational processes. Nevertheless, there are very real dangers if the sole criteria for evaluation revolve around issues of accountability and cost-effectiveness. We are warned by Hayward (1979) of the need to counterbalance administrative and mechanical structures with human and organic processes.

In nursing education the English National Board for Nursing, Midwifery and Health Visiting needs to be satisfied that schemes submitted for approval contain very specific plans for overall course evaluation. However, there are no national evaluative criteria, guidelines or models which schools of nursing can incorporate into their curriculum design. The following classification of evaluation models is one described by Lawton (1981), and an attempt will be made to identify from this classification those models that may appear compatible with the requirements for evaluating nursing courses.

The classical experimental model

This model relies heavily on quantifiable outcomes. A course employing the model will have very specific behavioural objectives which can be readily tested, and is likely to be based upon a cognitive taxonomy of educational objectives, i.e. Bloom (1956). Its name derives from the classical experiment whereby a process of pretesting, teaching programme, posttesting and control group comparison was employed. Such a model would have a use in courses that were heavily product-orientated and qualitative values had low importance. A model of this type is feasible in nursing education where the nine competences of Rule 18(1) of the Nurses, Midwives and Health Visitors Rules Approval Order 1983 (D H S S 1983) are precisely broken down into a large number of individual skills. A complex system of cross-referencing could link each of these skills to a particular behavioural objective which could then be tested. The result would be an accurate analysis of the number of discrete skills acquired and, therefore, behavioural objectives achieved, which could then be totalled to determine the degree of competency attainment. This would then have to be validated against a control group of students on a course that did not use this particular approach. It would seem to be a very mechanistic method of evaluation and loses a lot of its immediate appeal when it becomes apparent that little attention is given to the qualitative values of human feelings and attitudes, factors which are important in a course where the target group are human individuals, i.e. the patient/client.

The illuminative model

An alternative title for this evaluation model is the anthropological model. In direct contrast to the classical model, this provides for a qualitative account of the course. Empirical data are not sought: the main concern is with description and interpretation based upon observation and interview. The advocates of this model would claim that it provides a much wider perspective of the whole course as opposed to just the measurement of behaviour. Furthermore, it would appear compatible with the process approach to teaching and learning where experiential methods are employed. Critics of this model would point at its potential for subjectiveness – too much depends upon the interests and values of the observer. This may be a particular problem where the evaluator is also the course manager or tutor, for role conflict is likely to occur. Before this model can become acceptable to those who would prefer more formal methods, its rules of procedure and skills required to apply it need to be defined more clearly.

The briefing decision-makers' model

In this model the evaluator is usually an external agent who is 'briefed' to provide information for decision-makers. This method of evaluation must therefore be concerned with political issues and perspectives. There is no intention to infer that the evaluator simply produces for the decision-makers the answers or evidence that they are seeking; nevertheless, there needs to be an awareness of the purpose of evaluation within the context of the relationship between the decision-makers and the course. The evaluator must carry out his function according to the 'contract' he has undertaken to fulfil. Three types of evaluation are described by MacDonald (1976) relative to the evaluation function:

1   Bureaucratic.   The evaluator functions as a consultant working on behalf of a funding organisation, i.e. government agency. Information elicited from the evaluation report is intended to be used for policy decision-making.
2   Autocratic.   The evaluator functions as an expert adviser. He reports accurately on the educational merits of a course and expects his advice and recommendations to be accepted and implemented.
3   Democratic.   The evaluator functions as an information service. He collects data, interprets it and then presents it to the decision-makers. No recommendations are offered as part of this evaluation.

Despite the differences in approach and emphasis that these three styles offer, their broad aim is to enable the collection of material and data that will assist decision-makers to make better informed choices.

The teacher as researcher model

Within nurse education it is common practice for the teacher to a course to also carry out the evaluation, or part of it. This approach is advocated by Stenhouse (1975), who sees the teacher as both curriculum developer and evaluator. To function effectively in this dual role the teacher must be research-minded and apply research findings not only to his teaching but as part of his evaluation techniques. Again, the problems of subjectivity and role conflict must be raised when applying this model and, inevitably, it must be perceived as self-evaluation on the part of the teacher. A technique increasingly used in this self-monitoring model is that of 'triangulation' (Elliott & Adelman 1976). The teacher, student and observer discuss, analyse and compare their observations of the teaching and learning activity, whether it is a single lesson, course unit or the whole course.

A modified version of triangulation is often used in nursing courses where the clinical supervisor (ward sister), student and personal tutor (observer) evaluate a period of practical experience undertaken by the student nurse.

The case study model

A wide range of evaluation techniques are used in this model in order to obtain as complete an account as possible of the whole course, or course unit. It will therefore employ both quantitative and qualitative methods, which will include measurement, interviews, observations and the use of questionnaires. Because of its very nature, it would normally be carried out by an external agency and therefore will have significant cost consequences. An example of case study evaluation is that of employing an independent research body or organisation to evaluate a course or a component of a course. This may be appropriate when implementing a new scheme or modifying an existing scheme of training. The difference between this evaluation model and that concerned with briefing decision-makers resides not in its process but in its functional outcome. Although the outcomes are presented to decision-makers, the purpose of the case study is not necessarily commissioned in order for a decision to be made. It is more likely to be employed to confirm or support a decision that has already been taken and implemented.

Summary

By examining a number of different evaluation models it is apparent that an educational course as complex as nursing cannot be effectively evaluated by using just one model. Whilst educational factors are of prime concern in any nursing course, the political issues of service provision and staffing establishments cannot be ignored. Performance indicators that reflect both quantitative and qualitative measures in input and output terms are increasingly required by health authorities and their general managers as part of quality assurance programmes.

Whilst fully supporting the expressed need to obtain value for money and accountability in all aspects of public service, it is essential that general managers should recognise that quality can cost money. A more efficient use of that money is always possible but there comes a point at which efficiency cannot be increased and consequently any reduction of resources at that point will result in lowered quality. A summary of evaluation models is shown in Table 9.1.

The process of evaluation – who evaluates?

All the people involved in a course of education, both at the planning stage and during its implementation, ought to contribute to evaluation. The principal participants in any nursing course are the course teachers, the practical/clinical

Table 9.1 A summary of evaluation models

Evaluation model	Mode of evaluation	Function of the evaluation	Comments
Classical/experimental	Quantitative	Measurement of behaviour using precise behavioural objectives	An eclectic approach — does not consider broader course values
Illuminative (anthropological)	Qualitative	Description and interpretation based upon observation and interview	Danger of being subjective — role conflict
1 Briefing decision-makers'	Both quantitative and qualitative	Bureaucratic: — consultant	May be seen as providing decision-makers with the information they require
2 Briefing decision-makers'	Both quantitative and qualitative	Autocratic: — expert adviser	It is expected that the evaluation results will be acted upon
3 Briefing decision-makers	Both quantitative and qualitative	Democratic: — information service	Provides a detailed report without recommendations
Teacher as researcher	Both quantitative and qualitative	Dual role of both curriculum developer and evaluator	Use of triangulation ? Subjectivity ? Role conflict
Case study	Both quantitative and qualitative	Factual reporting	Expensive if using an external agency; may be used to confirm beliefs

supervisors or mentors, the students themselves and, most importantly, the patients or clients and their relatives. In addition to these main participants there are many secondary or supportive individuals who make an indirect contribution towards evaluation, either by being represented on the curriculum development team or through close working relationships with the key course participants.

Although the validating body, i.e. the National Board, requires all courses to be evaluated, it is only able to play an intermittent role in the process through its education officer, who may visit a health authority and its school of nursing on infrequent occasions either to 'inspect' prior to course reapproval or in a crisis situation. Ideally, all the relevant education officers ought to be able to spend at least two periods each year in their 'areas' of the schools of nursing. One visit would involve meeting teachers and clinical mentors during their discussions on curriculum application where teaching and assessment strategies were being debated. A further visit of immense value would be to join the curriculum development team at its evaluation meeting when it receives the analysis of a year's course work from all the contributors. Very rarely does an institution seek the advice of 'expert evaluators' not directly involved with the health authority, i.e. researchers or consultants/advisers. Such a service is, of course, costly in terms of financial outlay but it may be argued that such expenditure could be seen as an investment for the longer term.

The remainder of this chapter seeks to discuss the evaluation roles of the teacher, clinical supervisor, student, patient and the curriculum development team.

Course evaluation and the nurse teacher

The nurse teacher is often involved with the course from its conception to its conclusion. As an active participant at all stages, the teacher may be considered to have a subjective self-interest in its success but in reality, as Biott (1981) asserts, the teacher should not be denied the opportunity to fulfil the role of 'honest broker' on behalf of the organisation, i.e. the school of nursing. The nurse teacher, despite this self-interest, has or should have a professional desire to participate objectively in the evaluation of the course. Previous experience will tell the teacher that no course is educationally perfect and that constant modification and revision to structure, content and assessment is essential if a course is to be kept dynamic and responsive to students' needs. A big influence on nurse teachers involved in the field of evaluation has been the publication of the (then) Joint Board of Clinical Nursing Studies (1978). Probably for the first time, a national nursing education validating body had produced a detailed, prescriptive guide to conducting course evaluation. The structure of this evaluative tool consisted of a teacher checklist together with a self-questionnaire sufficiently flexible to allow for individual modification or adaptation.

There is far more to the teacher's role in course evaluation than self-evaluation questionnaires, important though these may be. It is valuable for the teacher to keep a weekly log of educational activities as the course progresses. Significant occurrences such as successful learning opportunities and experiences or,

Table 9.2 Course unit teacher evaluation grid

Evaluation method	Objectives relating to health concept	Objectives relating to nursing models	Objectives relating to nursing process	Course unit objectives summary
Teacher, self-evaluation				
Teacher's log				
Teacher–peer group discussion				
Teacher–student group discussion				
Analysis of course work — assessed				
Analysis of course work — unassessed				
Teacher's subjective evaluation				
Overall comments and observations				
Evaluation summary				

conversely, unsuccessful teaching strategies should be noted, together with a comment on future action where necessary. This approach is supported by Rowntree (1981) who advises that a record of this type will assist with a more systematic and objective evaluation of the course or its units.

A number of teachers are likely to contribute to a particular course, the teacher referred to as having the evaluation role is the person designated to lead or coordinate the teaching/learning activities for a course unit. As part of the coordination function the unit teacher must arrange for all the other teachers involved to participate in continuing group discussion. If each of these contributing teachers is also keeping a log of significant events then the pooling of information and its analysis will provide important evaluation material. The course or unit teacher must also meet the student group for the specific purpose of discussing feelings and opinions about course effectiveness and the group's perception of progress within the course. Inevitably, the students will refer to assessments and their outcomes during a discussion on evaluation and the teacher will need to have some very clear statements to make about the group performance linked to achievement of unit objectives as reflected by assessment work. Analysis of course work, whether it be assessed or not, will form part of the teacher's evaluation report.

It may be helpful to the teacher, and eventually to those involved in the total course evaluation, for an evaluation grid to be completed for each course unit, as shown in Table 9.2. The objectives on the horizontal part of the grid are just examples and other key topics can be substituted.

Course evaluation and the practical supervisor

Practical experience directly supervised by qualified nursing staff accounts for over 80 per cent of nursing courses and is correspondingly the most difficult area to evaluate. During the course each student may have as many as twelve or fifteen supervisors, each working as nursing specialists in their particular discipline. Learning objectives for each of the practical experiences will have been declared, and the supervisor's role is to provide opportunities for the student to achieve these objectives. No less significant is the supervisor's responsibility to ensure that the objectives are relative to the experience being provided and that they are achievable within the timescale available. For specific clinical teaching activities, the nurse supervisor can use the same evaluation questionnaire as that available to the nurse teacher, but this may not be advisabe as the 'teaching role' of the clinical nurse is that of facilitator of learning through providing the student with effective experiences. A questionnaire that elicits a qualitative response whilst having the potential to produce essential information of a type that can be used to keep the learning experiences and objectives dynamic would seem to be most appropriate.

Attention has been drawn previously to the employee status of the student and the inevitable workload that the student has to shoulder. The skilful ward sister will attempt to safeguard the student's educational interests and, indeed, utilise, where possible, each component of work as a learning experience.

Where systems of quality assurance are in operation at the clinical/patient level, the supervisor and nurse teacher have a mechanism for identifying the

Table 9.3   Comparison of learner time spent in different activities

Activity	Hospital 1		Hospital 2	
	Time spent (min)	% of total	Time spent (min)	% of total
Communicating with patients	5180	5.3	3690	5.9
Patient hygiene	19 210	19.8	13 420	21.5
Medication	5390	5.5	4060	6.5
Charts	5790	6.0	4230	6.8
Communicating with relatives	390	0.4	320	0.5
Housekeeping, cleaning	4030	4.1	2220	3.5
Serving food and drinks, clearing away	3960	4.0	3360	5.4
Errands	1070	1.1	880	1.4
Unoccupied	5460	5.6	2110	3.4
Ward reports	5440	5.5	3350	5.4
Private study	950	1.0	760	1.2
Tuition	1290	1.3	45	0.26

students' workload and the amount of time in learning situations. By using *Criteria for Care* in conjunction with workload study, a quantitative measure of student activity can be ascertained (Ball & Goldstone 1984). A specimen data sheet showing students' workload and teaching/learning time is shown in Table 9.3, together with an analysis of specific activities.

Just as the nurse teacher discusses the course progression with students and other teachers, so can the nurse supervisor. At ward team meetings the staff can review student progress, monitor the effectiveness of ward teaching programmes and identify learning problems met by students. At the end of each student's practical ward experience the supervisor must endeavour to ascertain the student's perception and appraisal of the learning environment that the ward has provided, particularly from a health promotion and nursing skills viewpoint. During the length of a course unit/module the nurse will have undertaken the supervisory role for a number of students and therefore should be able to reach informed conclusions. It ought to be possible to construct an evaluation grid for each course unit to be completed by the nurse supervisor for submission to the curriculum evaluation team (Table 9.4).

The main purpose of the evaluation grid is to assist the nurse supervisor to determine whether the practical experience is fulfilling the student's needs in addition to the course requirements. Again, the topics referred to on the horizontal axis of the grid are the author's preference and other topics can be introduced.

Table 9.4 Nurse supervisor's unit evaluation grid

Evaluation method	Key topics for evaluation			
	Health concepts	Nursing theory/models	Nursing process/skills	Other key topics
Questionnaire — self-evaluation				
Quality assurance analysis — student activity				
Peer discussion				
Student interviews				
Analysis of learning objectives				
Analysis of student progress reports				
Supervisor's comments, subjective evaluation				
Evaluation conclusions and proposed actions				

Course evaluation and the student

The student nurse is the main subject, centre of focus and sole purpose of nurse training courses. Is sufficient attention paid to her opinions, observations and criticisms of the course in terms of its content, application and assessment practices? Certainly, there is an increasing tendency to consult students as part of the process of course evaluation and this may take the form of group discussions, the completion of questionnaires and involvement in curriculum development and review.

It is now common practice for each student group to have a representative and for these representatives to meet at frequent intervals as a students' council or representative committee. One of the committee's main functions should be that of course review and evaluation, but in order to discharge this responsibility adequate advice and guidance are necessary. Without wanting to restrict students to narrow areas of comment, it is necessary to focus attention on relevant issues directly related to the curriculum. Although concerns about residential accommodation, hospital canteens and recreational facilities are important to some students and need to be debated, these should not impinge upon critical discussions of course progress and satisfaction.

Whilst the student representative committee is a formal body for gathering information relative to course evaluation, Hopson & Scally (1981) point out that informal feedback by way of casual comments from students cannot be ignored. The reported throwaway remark or overheard comment is often significant and a useful adjunct to data that are more formally collected. If students feel that they are a part of the course and its development, sharing in the ownership, they will not only work hard at making it a success but will seek to criticise its shortcomings whilst also praising its strengths. Students learn better when they feel that they have some control over the learning situation, claim Stanton et al (1980) in their work on courses for the development of social and life skills, an area of study not dissimilar to nursing.

Student nurses, therefore, not only have the right to participate in course evaluation but a responsibility to do so — a responsibility on behalf of those that follow on subsequent courses. Because students are involved in all aspects of the course they should contribute to providing information with which all components of the course can be evaluated.

The use of questionnaires is a popular way of eliciting opinion, both objective and subjective, about experiences undertaken in the practice setting and its associated study periods, i.e. study block or study days. When questionnaires are to be used it is necessary to choose an appropriate time and place for their completion, and if questionnaires are to have any merit they must be addressed in a considered manner by the students, who should be free from constraints of time. It is futile, therefore, to expect an evaluative questionnaire to have any worth if it is introduced to the students at the end of an allocation with the instruction: 'Before you dash off can you fill this in? It will only take two minutes. Thanks.'

In addition to the questionnaire technique, evaluation can consist of one-to-one discussion between the practical mentor and student, or in trios with the addition of the nurse teacher. If more than one student is undertaking practical experience on the ward or clinical area it should be possible for them to discuss the value of the experiences they have received and participated in. Student diaries or journals may be a valuable aid to evaluation, particularly when considering a period of a number of weeks — it is all too easy to base one's judgement on the most recent experiences whilst forgetting what happened in the early weeks of a practical placement.

Course evaluation and the patient

This aspect of curriculum evaluation is rarely, if ever, used and therefore very little information about it is available. Perhaps the problems inherent in conducting such an appraisal are too numerous and complex ever to allow it to become a regular feature of course evaluation. Nevertheless, it must be recognised as an ideal to work towards and should be advocated to course teachers and practical supervisors for serious consideration.

Some health authorities are adopting policies designed to offer all patients and clients 'a personal service' in a positive attempt to increase consumer satisfaction. Schools of nursing in those health authorities where the provision of a personal service is given high priority must build the concept into all course curricula, and the selective application of appropriate nursing models using the nursing process is an essential component in each curriculum strategy.

The quality of care given to patients can be measured by using such tools as Rush Medicine or its anglicised counterpart, Monitor, together with *Criteria for Care* (Ball & Goldstone 1984). Consumer satisfaction is even more difficult to assess than quality of care. The only guide that most authorities have is the number of complaints received from patients, ex-patients and relatives in contrast to the number of 'thank-you' letters. An attempt to measure patient satisfaction has been conducted by U M I S T (1985); however, this survey sought to cover all the aspects of a stay in hospital and only a small proportion of the questionnaire related to nurse–patient activity.

Perhaps nurse teachers and practical supervisors could, with the help of patients, design a questionnaire that might be relevant to a student nurse's interaction with and service to her patients. If a survey involving patients is being planned it should be remembered that the approval of the authority's ethical committee must first be obtained.

As patients become increasingly involved in their own care and take an interest in health promotion and maintenance it is feasible that they could play a more positive role in the student nurse's learning experience. When patients can understand the workings of a model of nursing and the nursing process then they should be able more readily to appreciate the student's educational objectives and assessment requirements.

Regrettably at the moment, only indirect indicators such as quality of care measures and patient satisfaction surveys can be used as pointers towards course evaluation.

Evaluation and the curriculum development team

Basic nurse education/training courses are very complex structures. During the period of the course, i.e. 3 to 3½ years, the student progresses through a number of course units, participates in a large range of clinical/practical placements, is supervised by as many qualified nurses, receives teaching inputs from a variety of nurse tutors/clinical teachers and at the same time provides a service for patients and clients. Very few vocational courses can make so many demands upon the student and, indeed, on those who contribute to the student's learning experiences. If the course is considered to be complex then how much more so is its evaluation? The roles of the teacher, practical supervisor, student, external agency and patient are all considered to contribute to course evaluation, and representatives of these course participants will probably be included in the curriculum development team. In the absence of any formal external evaluating body other than the National Board, it would seem appropriate that the team which designed, introduced and developed the course should also process its evaluation. Negative aspects of this arrangement are offered by Heathcote et al (1982) who suggest that the evaluator is already committed to the success of the course and that there could well be a tendency towards self-justification. Although she is talking about the single evaluator, the accusation could equally apply to a group. Whilst acknowledging the possibility of self-justification, more attention must be given to the benefits that accrue from the curriculum development team carrying out the evaluation. Curriculum development and evaluation must not be carried out in isolation or separately from each other: there is a close relationship between the two. This is recognised in a definition of evaluation suggested by Butler & Vaile (1984), which consists of two components: firstly, 'the setting of objectives and standards that act as indicators of how things should be done' and secondly 'the appraisal of how things actually are done in the light of set objectives and standards'. The curriculum development team can and should fulfil both roles of development and evaluation. Even more important, once an evaluation has been carried out there is the need and will to act upon the evaluation outcomes. This is clearly the function of the curriculum development team and is a responsibility that cannot be devolved to anybody else. This assertion is supported by James (1983) who advocates that those who need to learn from evaluation are those who plan, manage and teach the curriculum.

As curriculum studies become an increasingly significant subject in schools of nursing, an appropriate response is to create a senior educational post to carry out this function: it is a vital developmental requirement in the management of nurse education today. The person who fulfils the role must, in addition to participating as a key member of the development team in relation to curriculum evaluation, be an adviser and resource on all curriculum matters. Such an appointment, however, must not cause other nurse teachers to abdicate the duty of keeping abreast of all curriculum developments and issues within nurse education. The curriculum studies adviser will analyse the reports of those who have been directly involved in evaluation activities and present these to the development team when they meet as an evaluation forum at the end of each course unit. The main role of the team is then to debate the evaluation reports and propose appropriate responses to the issues that have been raised. Because

Table 9.5 Summary of course unit evaluation

| Evaluator | Key curriculum components | | | |
	Health studies	Models of nursing	Nursing process	Others
Tutorial staff				
Practical supervisors				
Student group				
External agent				
National Board Education Officer				
Patients/clients				
Identified problems/ issues				
Proposed solutions/ actions				

the membership of the team will reflect those groups involved in the different evaluation areas of the course unit, not only can they verify the overall evaluation report but they can also give their commitment to the actions decided.

An evaluation summary of each course unit may be represented by the grid shown in Table 9.5.

Equally as important as receiving evaluation data is the dissemination of proposed actions or curriculum modifications in response to the data. The team must ensure that its decisions on curriculum change are widely publicised to both students and course participants.

Summary and conclusions

The subjects of assessment and course evaluation are, with very few exceptions, dealt with in educational textbooks as separate items and, indeed, in separate chapters, from the other elements of the curriculum. Although this is understandable for purposes of clarity and discreteness, it does tend to isolate them from what should be a holistic approach to the description of curriculum design and development. Whilst criticising this tendency for authors to compartmentalise the various components of the curriculum, the authors are very conscious of having done this in the structure and presentation of these chapters.

Both assessment of student attainment and course evaluation must be seen as integral features of any course and not mere adjuncts to the content and teaching/learning strategies. At each stage of course design and planning conscious effort must be given to build-in appropriate assessment procedures and devise mechanisms for evaluating the outcomes in relation to the course unit goals and objectives. Childs (1985) goes so far as to suggest that an evaluation strategy ought to be outlined before the course content and its application is formalised. This becomes imperative where assessment and evaluation are more than just a summative appraisal of the student's overall attainment and the terminal conclusion of the course's worth.

It cannot be denied that carefully structured assessment and evaluation strategies are very time-consuming for all concerned, from the student to the curriculum development team, but it should be viewed as an economical investment that enables a course to be dynamic and responsive to the needs for change where necessary. What appears to be irrefutable is that courses in the future will find it extremely difficult to survive if they do not have as an integral feature assessment and evaluation strategies that are consistent with the goals and competences which the course seeks to achieve.

References

Ball J A & Goldstone L A (1984) *Criteria for Care*. Newcastle Polytechnic
Biott C (1981) In Smetherham D (ed) *Practising Evaluation*. Nafferton Books
Bloom B S (1956) *Taxonomy of Education Objectives*. Harlow: Longman
Butler J R & Vaile M S B (1984) *Health and Health Services* London: Routledge & Kegan Paul
Childs D (1985) *Psychology and the Teacher*, 4th ed. Eastbourne: Holt

Department of Health & Social Security (1983) *The Nurses, Midwives and Health Visitors Rules Approval Order 1983*. London, D H S S

Elliott J and Adelman C (1976) *Innovation at the Classroom Level*. Milton Keynes: Open University

Heathcote G *et al* (1982) *Curriculum Styles and Strategies*. F E U

Hopson P and Scally M (1981) *Lifeskills Teaching*. Maidenhead: McGraw-Hill

James M (1983) Course evaluation and curriculum development. *Nursing Times*, **10**(8), 83

Lawton D (1980) *The Politics of the School Curriculum*. London: Routledge & Kegan Paul

Lawton D (1981) In Gordon P (ed) *The Study of the Curriculum*. London: Batsford Academic

MacDonald B (1976) In Tawney D (ed) *Curriculum Evaluation Today*. London: Macmillan

Rowntree D (1981) *Developing Courses for Students*. Maidenhead: McGraw-Hill

Stanton G P *et al* (1980) *Developing Social and Life Skills*. F E U

Stenhouse L (1975) *An Introduction to Curriculum Development*. London: Heinemann

U M I S T (1985) *What the Patient Thinks — A Survey of Patients at Three Lincolnshire Hospitals*. Manchester: U M I S T

10
Developments in Nurse Education

This concluding chapter indentifies and discusses some of the influencing factors that have brought about change and development in nursing education during recent years. It is necessary that all nurses involved in the teaching and supervision of students should appreciate why and how nurse education has become what it is today and, more importantly, the role each can play in its further development. Nurses, midwives and health visitors are by far the largest manpower group within the Health Service and they inevitably experience the effects of any change within that Service, whether it be national, regional or local. Because student and pupil nurses often amount to 20 per cent of the total nursing manpower in a health district, it is reasonable to claim that any factor that affects the way care is delivered to patients must also have some influence on the development of nurse education. A most recent example of this can be seen in the implementation of D H S S circular HC(84)13 (D H S S 1984), more commonly known at hospital level as 'Griffiths'. The N H S management enquiry (D H S S 1983a), of which circular HC(84)13 was the end-product, made little or no reference to nurse education. The English National Board felt it necessary to write to all chairmen of regional and district health authorities giving guidelines for district health authorities about the implications for professional education/ training. Perhaps every general manager in the country can, with hand on heart, claim not to have intentionally affected nurse education; nevertheless, the application of general management principles with increased devolution of accountability, more efficient use of resources and an emphasis on performance in terms of quality as well as quantity must inevitably feature significantly in the planning, delivery and evaluation of nursing care. Student and pupil nurses are receiving their practical experience within this changing environment and, therefore, educational programmes must be adjusted to recognise such signifi- cant developments. Such an example of change or influence on nurse training. falls into the category of political and organisational development within the Health Service. There are two other major categories of development that could influence nurse training: professional or statutory factors and educational factors such as a new syllabus or an experimental scheme.

Professional and statutory developments and nurse education

During the latter part of the 1960s and throughout the 1970s the nursing profession in general, and nurse education in particular, was advocating a change in basic training from both a process and a product perspective. In 1970, the then Secretary of State, Richard Crossman, set up the Committee on Nursing and appointed Professor Asa Briggs as its Chairman with the following terms of reference:

> 'To review the role of the nurse and the midwife in the hospital and the community and the education and training required for the role, so that the best use is made of available manpower to meet present needs and the needs of an integrated Health Service.'

Nine years elapsed from the time of setting up this Committee to the taking of positive action by the Government in 1979 and the passing of the Nurses, Midwives and Health Visitors Act (1979), despite the fact that the Committee had produced its report in 1972 and the Government had accepted its main recommendations in 1974. As a result of the 1979 Act the establishment of the four National Boards took place, followed by the creation of the United Kingdom Central Council for Nurses, Midwives and Health Visitors (U K C C). These new statutory bodies replaced over a transitory period (1982) the then statutory bodies, i.e. the three General Nursing Councils, three Central Midwives' Boards, the Council for the Education and Training of Health Visitors and the Panel of Assessors for District Nursing.

The 1979 Act did not concern itself with the detail of reforming and restructuring education and training, leaving this to the new statutory bodies. Very little time elapsed before the U K C C Working Group 3 published a consultation paper which mooted such concepts as colleges of nursing and midwifery, 'protected employee' status for the student and one grade of nursing qualification (U K C C 1982). Some may say that this added nothing very new to the recommendations proposed by 'Briggs' (Committee on Nursing 1972): nevertheless, the majority of nurse educationists applauded these recommendations, seeing in them an opportunity for greater autonomy with less dependence on nursing service for funding, together with a reduced commitment to meet manpower requirements. Understandably, many senior nurse managers were not as enthusiastic about such proposals as the nurse teachers. The financial climate had changed to one characterised by cash limits and fixed budgets. Together with the thought of loss of control over nurse education, these proposals were distinctly unattractive to most chief nursing officers jealously protecting their traditional authority over schools of nursing. Despite this potential resistance from a substantial section of senior nurse management, teaching staff were speculating not about whether or not change would happen but on the degree to which it would take place. It was therefore with some dismay, and even disbelief, that nurse teachers received a U K C C circular in June 1984 that advised that for the foreseeable future no steps would be taken to restructure the

Table 10.1   Comparison between the major recommendations of the ENB consultation paper and those of the RCN Commission

Main issues	RCN recommendations	ENB recommendations
Parts of the Register	A single qualification, i.e. Diploma in Nursing. Studies with the appropriate speciality noted. Six speciality areas	The specialist part of the Register to remain with a distinction between RGN (hospital) and RGN (community)
Course design and length	First year — Foundation Course. Common body of knowledge, attitudes, skills. Specialise in third year	Common core First year (theory centred) Second year (application centred) Third year (practice centred)
Location of courses	Colleges of Further and Higher Education — outside NHS	Gradual formation of collaborative links with Colleges of FE/HE
Status of student	Totally supernumerary for entire course	Supernumerary for first two years
Nurse teachers	All teachers should be graduates. Teachers should carry clinical responsibility. Continue to be specific courses for preparation of nurse teachers	There should be a single category of nurse teacher. Graduates in the long term
Continuing education	'Professional development is essential to the maintenance of an effective nursing service'	'There should be continuing up-dating provision' 'There should be advanced courses'.
Unqualified staff	Too many assistants/auxilliaries	Care assistants with flexible roles combining skills of home helps and ward orderlies
Curricular features	Health promotion. Spiral curriculum, supervised practice 30 per cent. Specialisation in third year, supervised practice 50 per cent	Student-centred learning. Health promotion. Shifting theory/practice balance, one-third to two-thirds in second year. Choice of speciality in third year

provision for nurse education and that in organisational terms the status quo would remain, albeit that those schools which were developing relationships with colleges of further and higher education were to be encouraged. If 1984 was a year of gloom and despondency for those nurses seeking positive change and development within nurse training, then 1985 was to offer an abundance of potential for change with the production of a Consultation Paper by the English National Board, the publication of the Report of the R C N Commission and the announcement by the U K C C that it was to carry out an in-depth project to determine the preparation needed to enable nurses, midwives and health visitors to practise in the next decade and beyond. This quickly assumed the title of Project 2000. The Report of Project 2000, entitled *A New Preparation for Practice*, was published in May 1986 with an invitation to the profession to

Table 10.2   Summary of the recommendations of Project 2000

Project 2000: major recommendations	Similarity with other reports i.e. ENB, RCN, Briggs
Five parts of the Register — ADULT, CHILD, MIDWIFERY, MENTAL ILLNESS, MENTAL HANDICAP — through branching of course	ENB — six parts of Register, i.e. + health visiting RCN — six specialities of the Diploma to be noted
Common foundation programme of 2 years + 1 year branch programme — 3 years in total	ENB — common core + increasing speciality RCN — one year foundation course
Single list of competencies applicable to all registered practitioners	ENB — reference to the competences Rule 18(1) RCN — no specific reference to competences
Coherent, comprehensive and cost-effective framework of education beyond registration	ENB — strong yes to continue education RCN — continuing up-dating provision required
Specialist practitioners; some will be team leaders	ENB — Advanced Diploma studies in all specialities RCN — Advanced Diplomas in clinical specialities
Students should be totally supernumerary	ENB — supernumerary 2 years RCN — totally supernumerary
Aide to the nurse, a helper	ENB — care assistants RCN — fewer auxilliaries
Practitioners should have formal preparation for teaching in the practical setting	RCN — teachers of nursing should carry clinical responsibility ENB — no reference
Teaching qualifications at degree level for nurse teachers	RCN — all teachers of nursing should be graduates ENB — in the long term, all teachers should be graduates
Single level of nurse. Conversion courses for ENs	ENB — single level + conversion RCN — single level
Academic validation of nursing courses must be pursued	RCN — urges academic validation ENB — no specific reference to seeking academic validation

submit comments by the beginning of October 1986. Over 2500 submissions were duly received by the Council.

Both the English National Board's consultation paper and the R C N Commission Report *The Education of Nurses: A New Dispensation* (Judge Report, 1985) contributed substantially to the content of Project 2000 and to the profession's analysis and commentary of its recommendations. The major recommendations of these two reports, i.e. the E N B and R C N, are summarised in Table 10.1 so that a quick comparison can be drawn between them and the developments proposed by Project 2000 (Table 10.2).

Understandably, each of the three reports has certain unique elements that distinguishes it from the others. There is a substantial amount of common ground, albeit with differences of emphasis on particular issues, i.e. the degree of supernumerary status. All three reports, however, are in unison on the matter of the necessity to provide for the changing role of the nurse to meet the changing health needs of the nation. The English National Board's consultation paper makes the following statement:

> 'The health care needs and expectations of society change over time and the role of the professional carer changes and develops to meet these needs and demands. Professional education and training courses cannot remain static and those responsible for approving institutions to provide courses must be sensitive and responsive to changing reality. At the present time the strategic plans for health care being developed by Health Authorities will reflect these needs and must be matched by strategic proposals for education and training courses.'

The Royal College of Nursing's Commission on Nursing Education makes a similar claim for change, but does it with a 'tongue in cheek' approach:

> 'The layman will need to be convinced that anything very much is wrong. He is likely to believe that the nurse in our society may indeed be undervalued and underrewarded, but not that she is irresponsible or ill-prepared. His experience suggests that the public has confidence in the quality of practical nursing, and prompts the question 'If the system of training is wrong, why are its products so good?' He will, moreover, be disposed in a spirit of traditional Anglo-Saxon pragmatism, to favour a system which embeds training in practice and eschews fancy notions or theories of "Education". He will be sceptical of any attempts to move the training of nurses from its present base. He will, if pressed, want his bedside nurse to be trained and practical rather than educated and questioning.'

Project 2000 describes in detail the changing health needs of the nation and examines health and social trends as they are now and how they may develop over the next decade:

> 'The N H S is already undergoing an unprecedented level of critical scrutiny and review. In the current economic circumstances it is right that this should be so. We believe that critical scrutiny must now be turned on the relationship between education and service, to find a new basis on which to go forward towards the new century. We believe that the time has come for a new service/education contract, one which can better serve the N H S. In today's straitened circumstances, every profession is likely to be asked to take a fresh look at its past practices and to find new ways of working. The new structure of nursing, midwifery and health visiting has provided an unprecedented opportunity for a review such as this one, and practitioners at all levels have welcomed and endorsed it.'

How can the future role of the nurse be described? To many people, particularly those members of the general public who have never spent any time

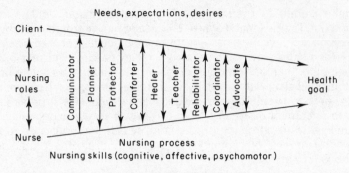

Fig. 10.1   Conceptual representation of the nursing role

in hospital, the nurse is a well-established stereotype characterised by crisply starched uniforms, white aprons and hair tightly gathered under frilly lace caps. Nursing, equally stereotyped, consists of making beds, straightening pillows, taking temperatures and administering medicines. Describing the nursing role using such criteria is, one hopes, no longer appropriate; nevertheless, Douglas (1982) refers to it as the *normative* role, i.e. that concept held by the lay person. Less of a stereotype, but still recognisable within the nursing membership of the Health Service, is the nursing role described in terms of *situational* criteria. This role is characterised by the situation in which the nurse is working: hence, we get the 'surgical sister', 'geriatric nurse', 'casualty sister' and 'outpatients nurse'. Each will have had the same basic training but through working in a particular situation with a particular client group have adopted and adapted techniques and behaviours to best suit that situation. The nursing role which takes situational criteria as its parameters is more flexible than that using normative criteria. There is room for change and adjustment: the nurse caring for a patient in hospital has to adopt a different role if she is required to follow up that patient's care as an outpatient after discharge. Two further sets of criteria are described by Douglas which identify and develop the nursing role. The *functional* criteria do not restrict the nursing role to stereotypes or situations but are concerned with the activities that are carried out by the nurse, i.e. carer, teacher, investigator, planner, advocate. Such functional criteria do not only allow role change to occur but they positively facilitate change. Patient-centred care, a holistic approach, and provision of a personal service are no longer clichés. Nurses actively practise many of these care concepts which recognise the patient and his relative as partners in caring contracts. Such a nursing role (Fig. 10.1) using *interactional* criteria takes into account the patient's own role with its attendant needs and expectations. These last two sets of criteria, i.e. functional and interactional, are increasingly evident, and as the nursing role expands in response to new health problems and society's requirements they are very necessary for the development of nursing. Inevitably, the way in which student nurses are prepared for the nursing roles of the future has also to undergo change.

Historically, the study of nursing has adopted the physical and social sciences as its knowledge base, but this has undergone a substantial change in recent years, influenced to a large extent by nursing research and scholarship both in this country and in the United States. This academic interest to describe nursing and offer conceptual models as directives for practice seems to be doing two things. Firstly, nurses are being encouraged to perceive nursing practice as something other than an extension of medicine and they are, therefore, questioning the medical model as an efficient and effective approach to care delivery. Secondly, in order to substantiate and consolidate these new approaches to care nurses are becoming more and more anxious to receive continuing learning opportunities. In response to this demand, health authorities are rapidly developing departments of continuing education and in-service training within their schools of nursing.

Increasing numbers of young people with sound educational backgrounds have entered the Health Service, bringing with them questioning and critical attitudes. They have revealed as unacceptable some of the values that earlier nurses had traditionally clung to. Because these nurses are eager to examine psychological and sociological issues of health care in addition to technical and pathological studies, a more humanistic and holistic awareness of the patient is emerging and many courses of preparation for nurses are now adopting a nursing model approach with primary and team care delivery. The increasing knowledge base that underpins these practices is novel and in most cases yet to be researched; however, it is itself a secondary stimulus for continuing education.

As nursing courses redress the balance between training and education, together with the emergence of a new body of research-based knowledge, perhaps nurses may be in a better position to claim that what was an occupation is now becoming a profession – the final transition from 'knowing that . . . ' to 'knowing how . . . '. Nursing roles in the future are, one hopes, destined to undergo change and expansion, with little risk of stereotypes occurring as they have in the past. Whatever roles are practised, the need for education is now very much accepted and the next decade will see specific developments in role preparation for nurses as a continuation of basic nurse education.

Political and organisational developments and nurse education

Reference was made to political and organisational changes influencing the development of nurse education at the beginning of this chapter and the implementation of the recommendations of the N H S management enquiry (Griffiths) was used as an example of a change influencing nursing education.

Ten years earlier, the 1974 reorganisation of the Health Service brought about fundamental changes in the way that nursing education was managed and organised. Although the holders of the newly created posts of Director of Nurse Education were still accountable to the Chief Nurses or District/Area Nursing Officers, far greater responsibility was devolved than had hitherto been the case and the Director of Nurse Education was directly accountable to the statutory body (G N C) for the education budget. Increasingly, the Director of Nurse Education played a significant role in the formulation and planning of nursing policy within the health authority alongside nursing service managers.

Although during the late 1960s and early 1970s some nurse training schools had combined as hospital management committees underwent 'grouping', the 1974 reorganisation required the further amalgamation of smaller schools of nursing, often single discipline, into district or area schools, which in most cases offered training for more than one part of the then Register and Roll. This brought together teaching staff from the different nursing disciplines and enabled them to contribute their particular knowledge and skills to the development of the new educational structure, particularly if the 'new' school was on one site. However, where the different departments of a district/area school of nursing remained on geographically separate sites, the phenomena of 'mini schools' within the larger organisation persisted for many years. Another important feature of educational development during the decade from 1974 to 1984 was the incorporation of postbasic and continuing education and in-service training into the sphere of responsibility of the schools of nursing. A major spin-off from this development was the marked increase in education and service relationships, both in liaison and collaborative terms. It may be a gross generalisation to claim that nurse teachers began to spend more of their time in clinical areas and that ward sisters became increasingly involved in school-based educational activities. The Joint Board of Clinical Nursing Studies (J B C N S) had been established to promote postbasic education through the production of outline curricula for a wide spectrum of clinical specialties and the approval of courses within health authorities and higher education. More will be said of the development of postbasic and continuing education in a later part of this chapter, under the heading of educational and curricular developments. Organisationally, schools of nursing developed markedly in the period from 1974 to 1980, with the Director of Nurse Education being required to become far more of a manager than the previous roles of Principal Nursing Officer (Training/Education) and Principal Tutor had necessitated. Many directors began to seek control of the student and pupil nurse salary budgets and, by virtue of that, had the last say in where learners were allocated for practical experience. With the increased autonomy that schools began to enjoy came the need for better administrative and non-teaching support. Larger schools were able to appoint general administrators to manage the secretarial and clerical functions; qualified librarians and audiovisual aids technicians have tended to become the rule rather than the exception, enhancing educational and teaching resources.

On a political level, the Government had set up a Royal Commission in the Health Service and its report entitled *Patients First* initiated the onset of a further period of change, this time to be referred to as 'restructuring' of the Health Service, as opposed to reorganisation. Unlike the 1974 reorganisation, *Patients First* was concerned totally with the structure and management of the provision of a Health Service to patients. Health Circular HC(80)8 (D H S S 1980) advised on the implementation of the restructuring and was very specific that all authorities should ensure that existing arrangements for nurse education would continue, undisturbed as far as possible. There were very definite implications for schools of nursing, even though nursing education was not part of the new management structure. Whereas a director of nurse education may have had to liaise with four divisional nursing officers under the 1974 structure, this number had now doubled in many cases under their new title of Directors of Nursing

Services. A typical problem for nurse teachers as a result of the creation of health care units was that of uniformity and consistency. Previously a number of general hospitals providing practical experience placements for student nurses would have been managed by one divisional nursing officer and nursing policies, procedures and practices would have been fairly consistent throughout all the hospitals. With four directors of nursing services replacing the one divisional nursing officer, each applying different policies, procedures and practices in their particular hospital or health care unit, there is, understandably, much scope for confusion among students and concern among teachers.

Very quickly on the heels of *Patients First*, the Government asked Sir Roy Griffiths of Sainsbury's, the supermarket chain, to lead an enquiry team which would be able to advise the Secretary of State on 'the management action needed to secure best value for money and the best possible service to patients'. The enquiry commenced in February 1983 and the team published its report in October of the same year (D H S S 1983a).

Since the 1974 reorganisation, the management style at all levels, i.e. regional, area, district and division or unit, had been that of consensus, with doctors, nurses and administration having equal status and authority within management teams. Whilst Griffiths advised that the best aspect of consensus management be retained, he urged that the general manager principle of private industry and commerce ought to be adopted, thus reducing delays in decision-making and elevating the status of decisions made above common denominator level. The Secretary of State speedily accepted the recommendations of the Griffiths team and implementation got under way in 1984.

Again, it might appear that, as was assumed with *Patients First* in 1980, the Griffiths recommendations of 1984 would have little significant effect upon schools of nursing. Many nurse educationists would argue that the combination of these two factors has had more influence on the organisation and management of nursing education than any other event since the 1974 N H S reorganisation. The years since 1980 have seen much emphasis on accountability and performance, particularly at managerial level. Cash limits, performance indicators, Rayner scrutinies, value for money, may be jargon terms at the moment to many Health Service employees, but to the manager at district, unit and ward level, and that most certainly includes the ward sister, the terms have reality and their meaning and application has to be fully understood and practised.

As a result of the implementation of the general management function, a number of models of accountability have emerged that have drastically changed the conventional role of the Director of Nurse Education. Many directors are still professionally and managerially accountable to the 'chief nurse' within the health authority. This person may have one of many titles ranging from District/Chief Nursing Officer to Director of Patients Services or Director of Quality Assurance. The last two titles are significant in that the word 'nurse' does not appear, thus posing the question: 'Need they be filled by a member of the nursing profession?' An increasing number of D N E roles are being amalgamated with that of District Nursing Adviser where the post-holder is accountable to the District General Manager. A more complicated model is that of Director of Nurse Education and District Education and Training Officer, i.e. responsible for all nursing education/training and the in-service/continuing education and training of other professional and employee groups. In this capacity the post-holder may be accountable to the 'chief nurse' for all nursing, midwifery and health visiting education/training and to the District Personnel Officer for the training of other employee groups — an example of joint accountability that is increasingly common within general management practice. Such appointments would appear to be quite practical and realistic within a totally Health-Service-controlled environment, but are very much incompatible with the increasing desire of nurse education to move into the field of higher education. Nurse educationists, however, cannot have it both ways — they cannot enjoy the academic respectability of employment in higher education and at the same time play a significant role in the planning and development of a district health authority's nursing and patient care policy.

Educational and curricular development in nursing education

To appreciate current developments in nursing education from an educational and curricular perspective it is necessary to reflect back over some of the more significant changes of the recent past. During the 1970s, modular or semi-modular schemes were the fashion and today in the later part of the 1980s many courses of basic nursing are of the modular type. A module is, by definition, a self-contained piece or segment of a larger whole and in nurse training it was characterised by a period of practical experience sandwiched between prepara-tory and consolidatory study blocks. The three years' training comprised a series of such modules running in linear fashion, and although some of the subject matter of the syllabus ran as a thread through all modules, to all intents and purposes the modules could be interchanged without a detrimental effect on the educational nature of the course. Another educational factor in vogue at this time was the preparation of behavioural objectives for all teaching and learning experiences both in the practical setting and in the classroom. These objectives were very detailed, and therefore numerous, commonly listed under the three headings of knowledge, skills and attitudes. The statutory body was very keen that ward sisters and other nursing service personnel should be involved in the preparation and development of these behavioural objectives. The criteria for successful completion of a module was the attainment of the learning objectives and not the level of attendance although, of course, excess sickness and absence had to be made up in overall terms.

A major reference document for nurse teachers and their service colleagues to use when preparing learning objectives was the General Nursing Council's (1974) circular 74/8/16. For those nurses who thought 'nursing competences' were novel to Rule 18(1) of the Nurses, Midwives and Health Visitors Rules Approval Order (D H S S 1983b) it may be a surprise to discover that the G N C had, almost a decade earlier (1974) published *A Specification of Nursing Competence*, recommending them to teaching staff when considering objectives of training. This 'specification' was the work of an *ad hoc* committee of the G N C set up to consider the future pattern of examinations and assessments. In attempting to do this, the Committee felt it necessary to specify what was meant by competence in nursing. Using the model of the nursing process, competency was described in terms of the nurse's ability to carry out 'observation', 'interpretation', 'planning', 'action' and 'evaluation'. Whilst defining nursing competency for each of these elements the Council still felt it necessary to break the competency down into very specific details of observation, interpretation, planning and action. For example, under nursing competency of interpretation of observations the circular listed the fourteen items of Virginia Henderson's Basic Nursing Component. On reflection, perhaps, it was appropriate to go into such detail as models of nursing were rarely used, indeed unknown to the majority of nurses. Although the 'Briggs' Committee on Nursing had reported in 1974, there was an absence of decision from the Government. At the same time the European Economic Community had published its nursing directives. There was a very real need for the G N C to provide some fairly urgent guidance on educational policy. Such guidance was offered in circular 77/19, *A Statement of Educational Policy*, July 1977. This document sought to identify a number of important considerations for those nurses and teachers involved in nursing education when planning and developing curricula. Changes in patterns of health and illness, society's expectations of health care and the changing needs of society were highlighted for consideration. The characteristics of both a satisfactory educational setting and of a framework for the development of curricula were specified. Finally, guidance was provided for those schools of nursing who were in the process of designing curricula. In this last section of the circular, the Council reminded nurses' teachers of the nine component abilities specified in the E E C nursing objectives. These component abilities are not dissimilar from the 'competences' of the 1974 circular, nor those of Rule 18(1). Again, the nursing process was offered as a 'unifying thread for the study of patient care and as a framework for nursing practice'.

The training and education of nurses, midwives and health visitors is inextricably linked with the changes and developments that take place in health care delivery both in hospital and community services. Curricula must be dynamic in order to respond to and accommodate change in nursing practice, but there comes a time when the syllabus from which the curriculum is derived no longer suffices in meeting the demands of such changes — the syllabus has become out of date. This was recognised to be the case in both mental illness and mental handicap nurse training during the late 1970s, where a substantial shift in emphasis from institutional models of care and treatment to preventive measures with community and day-care facilities providing primary care services. New syllabuses for mental illness and mental handicap nursing courses were published in 1982 (G N C 1982a, 1982b), with a requirement that they be implemented by all schools of nursing with such courses no later than 1987. This may have seemed an inordinate length of time for implementation but an educational change as fundamental as a new syllabus has far-reaching implications. When designing a curriculum from a new syllabus in nursing as opposed to a vocational course in further education, one of the first criteria to consider is the ability of the health services within the health authority to fulfil the demands of the new syllabus. Such factors to be considered are the learning experience placements. Are they adequate in both quantity and quality? Are there plans for service development? Do qualified nursing staff possess skills in modern care practice and are they willing to increase further their knowledge through continuing education? Most importantly, is the health authority willing to invest increasingly scarce resources in educational development and change?

Educational development is usually gradual and undramatic, which cannot really be said of the recent surge in demand for increased opportunities to update, refresh and participate in aspects of continuing education and training. The need for this has always been recognised and many health authorities have, albeit in a superficial way, attempted to create in-service training programmes. These, in the main, have tended to be *ad hoc* in nature rather than planned, purposeful strategies designed to meet both the needs of the nursing staff and, perhaps more importantly, the needs of the services required by the consumer, i.e. the patient.

Throughout the 1970s, postbasic clinical nursing courses had been approved in many schools of nursing by the Joint Board of Clinical Nursing Studies (J B C N S), but the 1980s saw a marked proliferation of specialist courses, now validated by the National Boards. With this development in postbasic education, the majority of schools of nursing have been given the total responsibility for all educational and training developments within their district, and specific Departments of Continuing Education or In-service Training headed by a Senior Tutor or Assistant Director of Nurse Education have been created in schools. There seems to be no single cause for this major thrust in the direction of continuing education, the success of which is even more remarkable in view of the financial restrictions imposed on the public sector.

Educational change during the 1980s has been mainly in the area of curriculum studies, with significant developments in the assessment and examination of students and the evaluation of courses. Curricular planning and development teams have been demanded by the statutory bodies, and effective evaluation has become a vital part of the Boards' strategy for the reapproval of courses. Schools of nursing have responded to these challenges and, in particular, nursing service staff, i.e. ward sisters, have developed very real skills in curricular planning, particularly where courses have an experiential emphasis. A few schools of nursing have been able to allocate some of their resources to the creation of senior teaching posts dedicated either solely or partly to curricular studies. Where this has been possible it should not be allowed to remove from other teaching staff the responsibility of contributing to curricular matters and keeping abreast of developments in the field of curricular study.

Just as there has been an interest in the emergence of models of nursing so, too, has keen attention been paid to curricular models when planning new or revised education courses. Comment has been made earlier in this chapter on modular schemes of training where a course consisted of a series of links in a chain. Such a course would most likely have been based upon a linear curricular model, where many topics were dealt with within a module before proceeding to the next module where a different set of topics was to be studied. This type of curricular model is now being replaced, in many instances, by the spiral curricular model. Rather than complete the study of a particular item before moving on to a new topic, the spiral curriculum offers the student the opportunity to examine a range of subjects at a particular stage or level of the course and then, as the course progresses, the subjects are further examined either from a different perspective or at a higher level. For example, the subject of 'pain' may be studied at an early stage of the course from a physiological aspect — part of the healthy person's physical response to certain stimuli. In the subsequent stages of the course 'pain' may be reexamined from a diagnostic or pathological perspective, whilst at another level it may be considered from an emotional and spiritual viewpoint. A characteristic of the spiral curriculum is that each time a topic is 'revisited' it is built up, expanded and reinforced, so that at the completion of the course it has become part of the student's new knowledge or skill repertoire.

Developments in curricular design

Much attention and effort has been devoted by statutory bodies and curricular planning teams to promote the integration of theory and practice, or as some prefer it, concurrent theory and practice. It seems a very difficult phenomenon to guarantee, particularly if the people teaching theory have little or no contact with those providing and supervising the practice, and more so if the theory precedes the practice. The proponents of experiential teaching and learning will only provide theory for a student if it can be used immediately in a practical way, and in most learning situations the student will undergo the experience prior to receiving the associated theory.

Health model

Reference has already been made to Rule 18(1) which describes nine sets of competences that a qualified nurse must attain and practice. The first of these states that the nurse will ' . . . advise on the promotion of health and the prevention of illness'. Any curriculum that seeks to prepare a student to fulfil this function will need to contain a substantial health studies component. It may be the case that the curricular planning team would seek to base the whole content of the curriculum on a health model rather than on the traditional illness model. The study of health must go far beyond the physiological perspective, important as this is, and address the issues of the politics and economics of health, spiritual and emotional health, sociocultural concerns for health and the health — ill-health continuum. Students should be encouraged at an early stage in the course to appreciate the concept of health in the broadest sense and develop a commitment to its promotion, education and maintenance. If the student's own experiences of health, and those of friends and relatives, can be utilised in the learning process it may follow that the student can more readily appreciate what causes ill-health and disease. After all, the care and treatment of ill people and their diseases is a fundamental part of the nursing role.

Common core

There are three main types of basic nursing course: general nursing, nursing the mentally ill and nursing the mentally handicapped, i.e. Part 1, 3 and 5 of the

Register. The nursing of children can be studied alongside general nursing on a comprehensive course leading to registration on both Parts 1 and 8 of the Register. All these basic nursing courses, irrespective of which part of the Register they lead to, have many similarities in curricular content. There are readily identifiable areas of both theory and practice that are common to all nursing courses and, whilst the emphasis may be slightly different, the commonality is sufficiently strong to make it seem odd that students on courses leading to differing parts of the Register study these common subjects in isolation from each other. The English National Board's Consultation Paper (1985) advocated there should still be courses leading to different parts of the Register but proposed that each course should have a common core. Students on different courses would 'share' the common core and learn together, and the subjects would include:

— Health studies: promotion, maintenance, education
— Models of care and nursing process
— Biological and behavioural sciences
— Research appreciation and application
— Social sciences
— Information technology

The application of this common core material to specialist areas of care would be developed in specific modules pertaining to the discipline being studied.

Common foundation programme

The U K C C's Project 2000 Report (1986), *A New Preparation for Practice*, recommends a common foundation programme. The Report advocates that there should be basic education courses for separate parts of the Register, four parts in this case, not the seven recommended by the English National Board Consultation Paper. The four parts would be mental illness, mental handicap, the adult and the child. Whereas a common core enables students from all courses to share in the study and practice of a number of predetermined subjects and their application, the common foundation programme requires all students on all courses to undertake the same initial preparation irrespective of their eventual nursing specialty.

Project 2000 describes the common foundation programme as the fundamental building block on which all further preparations will be based. The health 'model' approach is considered essential for a foundation programme, reflecting the stated goals of the National Health Service in terms of teaching self-care, promoting independent living and providing a personal service that respects the patient as an individual. A further feature of the programme will be the need in addition to theoretical studies, for practice in a wide range of settings with a variety of care groups. During these experiences the student will gain insights to many different health care situations and observe other professional groups in practice. The final purpose of the common foundation programme is to prepare all students for further learning in their chosen branch programme, i.e. the nursing specialty in which each has chosen to practice. Normally, students will enter the course with a distinct idea of which specialty they wish to qualify in. However, it is possible with a foundation programme to delay that decision or change a preference before the specialist branch programmes commence, subject, of course, to the number of places available within each branch programme. An optimum length for an initial common foundation programme could be in the region of eighteen months to two years, the latter period being the original suggestion of Project 2000, with branch programmes of one to one-and-a-half years.

Developments in curricular application

Schools of nursing and other educational institutions

Liaison and collaboration between schools of nursing and further and higher education establishments is not a new phenomenon. There have been effective links for many years through such activities as the Diploma in Nursing, prenursing courses, art-of-examining courses, management training and, in recent years, both combined courses and nursing degrees. More recently, there has been collaboration between schools of nursing and higher education colleges at the basic nurse training level. In 1985 the English National Board approved a small number of pilot schemes in general nursing which would, in effect, test a whole range of curricular and organisational initiatives ranging from health models and college-based studies to supernumerary status and inbuilt professional development. Whilst the Royal College of Nursing Commission's report advocated the wholesale transfer of nursing education into the higher education sector, the English National Board and, more recently, the United Kingdom Central Council, urge development of relationships and collaborative links, the latter statutory body publicly recognising that students, even when supernumerary, will still on average contribute some 20 per cent of their time to nursing service.

To many practising nurses and nurse teachers the issue of most concern when debating the merits or otherwise of nurse education being based in higher education institutions is that of the status of the nursing qualification. In the past, registration as a nurse after a three-year course has had little or no academic value or acknowledgement despite the fact that most schools of nursing demand a minimum entry of five O levels. No credit is allowed by universities or polytechnics towards degree studies and 'nurse registration' on its own does not allow automatic entry to higher educational courses.

Increasing numbers of ward sisters, midwives, district nurses and health visitors undergo further and higher education, the last two groups, of course, receiving their professional postbasic training in higher education. In addition to the traditional courses already mentioned, i.e. Diploma in Nursing, art-of-examining, etc., there are many other opportunities for education and professional development. The City and Guilds Further Education Teachers Certificate (Course 730) has always been popular. Courses validated by the Institute of Health Service Management are proliferating and attracting nurse managers and clinicians to their ranks, in addition to adminstrators and paramedical heads. The advantages of developing close links with a college or polytechnic are numerous and include the use of such resources as an academic library, laboratories and computer facilities, but equally importantly, the opportunity to interact with other professionals and participate in the sharing of ideas, opinions, values and beliefs.

Having said that the nursing qualification in its own right has little academic respectability, it is none the less significant to overhear a senior lecturer from a college of higher education involved in nurse education, who regularly gives a week of his interterm holiday to working on the wards as part of his orientation to the Health Service, express admiration at the depth of knowledge, the decision-making skills and the teaching ability of the qualified nurses who he works alongside. Collaboration in its true sense implies a relationship in which both parties have something to offer each other. The relationship between a school of nursing and higher education seems to assume a one-way flow of provision in that the college is the provider of educational services or resources and the school plays the role of grateful recipient, often paying handsomely for the service. There is no reason why the traffic in educational and professional services should not be two way. Health authorities and their schools of nursing can provide a wide range of expertise in such fields as first-aid training, health promotion and education, counselling skills, measurement of performance, management training and a whole variety of practical experience placements for students on college/polytechnic courses. There is much opportunity and scope for profitable relationships to develop between the Health Service and educational institutions, with each still being able to retain their respective and respected professional identities.

Integrating education and service — the joint appointee

Nurse teachers' opinions seem to be divided on who is the best person to teach nursing in the practical or clinical setting. Is she the nurse teacher who has kept 'up-to-date' with practical nursing skills and their application or is she the practising nurse who has had some preparation in the skills of teaching, supervising and assessing? Who does the ward sister think is the most appropriate person to teach patient-centred care? Can a nurse teacher, even one who has kept abreast of practical nursing developments, have the credibility for teaching applied nursing care when he or she is not actually charged with the responsibility for the management of patients and their care? These are just a few of the questions that practising nurses and nurse teachers must somehow resolve and reach agreement on. The joint appointment seeks to combine the best that each has to offer, i.e. ward sister and nurse teacher. Whilst there are many variations on the theme, the typical joint appointee is either a nurse tutor or clinical teacher who is appointed to fulfil the role of ward sister. Whilst having complete accountability for the patients and their care this person is responsible for providing a high standard of learning opportunities and effective teaching programmes for students and other nursing staff allocated to the ward. The joint appointee may be provided with additional support, in the form of a junior sister or an additional staff nurse, to compensate for the dual role and additional workload. Experience shows that unless a person in a joint appointment post has adequate qualified nursing support either of two extreme situations will tend to occur. At one extreme the post-holder is so 'thinly spread' between managing the staff and patient care and attempting to create, supervise and facilitate learning experiences that both areas end up with less than adequate provision. The other extreme finds the joint appointee so involved and committed to giving maximum effort to both aspects of the job that a 45- to 50-hour working week is no exaggeration.

A variation on the joint appointment theme which seems to escape the problems of the ward-based post is that where the nurse/teacher is not a site manager, e.g. ward sister, but has a functional role, i.e. health visitor, community psychiatric nurse or nurse specialist. In this capacity the joint appointee may have a modified caseload or fulfil an advisory or consultancy-type role in addition to providing an educational service at basic, postbasic and continuing education levels. Because the person is not responsible for managing a ward or department together with subordinate staff it is easier to plan and manage workload and responsibility; there is a greater scope for flexibility in the working day.

Distance and open learning

These aproaches to learning are becoming increasingly popular with nurses. For those health care professionals who want to participate in continuing education at their own pace and in a mode they feel best suited to, distance learning offers a solution. It is not a new approach to education: distance learning has been around for many years in the form of correspondence courses and the Open University. By definition, the student of distance learning participates at home or away from the origin or source of the programme, although in most types of distance learning some attendance may be required at a centre such as a polytechnic or university; however, this is always a minor proportion of the whole course of study. The attractions for qualified nurses are: the flexibility of pace of learning; ability to study at home; the use of a wide range of media materials; the facility for repetition of 'difficult' areas; and, perhaps, the economy in terms of travelling and studying when not on duty if study leave is not available.

The terms 'distance' and 'open' learning are virtually interchangeable, there being little or no differentiating criteria, although the discerning may claim that open learning is carried out totally under the individual's own control whereas some distance learning is controlled by an educational institution, with required attendance.

Examples of the types of material available for study purposes range from learning packages on the management of patient care to interpersonal skills. There are two specific organisations currently producing open learning materials for nurses; one of these, the Distance Learning Centre, is based in the Polytechnic of the South Bank, London, and the second, Continuing Nurse Education has twin sites — Barnet College and Central Manchester College. All are part of the Open Tech Project, established and funded by the Manpower Services Commission.

Health PICKUP and N H S Training Authority

The National Health Service Training Authority was set up in 1983 for the purpose of enabling the N H S to assume full and direct responsibility for its own training. It incorporated into its structure the then National Staff Committees, the National Education Centres and the two N H S Training Centres. It must be emphasised that the N H S Training Authority is not concerned with basic professional education and training; nor does it have any direct relationship or influence on statutory bodies for education and training.

The Department of Education and Science (DES) launched in 1982 a scheme entitled PICKUP, standing for Professional, Industrial and Commercial Updating. Basically the concept is a simple one, designed to enable individuals to keep abreast of skills development in the professional, industrial and commercial arenas. Although some initial funding was necessary in the form of 'pump-priming', it was planned that PICKUP would be paid for by the customer at market prices.

Early in 1986 the Department of Education and Science, in conjunction with the National Health Service Training Authority, announced a major new programme of continuous professional education and updating for staff employed within the Health Service. This was named Health PICKUP and jointly funded at £½ million to get if off the ground. The development budget was seen to be necessary in order to analyse systematically the competences involved to ensure high standards of course design and to promote the development of new learning materials. Courses were envisaged as being modular and would, it was hoped, lead to formal academic awards. They are aimed at nine key professional groups within the N H S: nurses, midwives, health visitors, physiotherapists, speech therapists, clinical psychologists, occupational therapists, orthoptists, chiropodists. The training forum is one in which the N H S managers, professional bodies, Department of Education and Science, colleges, polytechnics and universities work together.

After identifying and analysing the skills required of all the different health care professions, it appeared that there were five broad areas: clinical skills, management skills, interpersonal skills, communication skills and teamwork skills. These were seen as vital elements in dealing with the major health issues, irrespective of professional boundaries.

Developments in nurse education — the future

The United Kingdom Central Council, set up by Act of Parliament, is charged by that Act to improve standards of nursing and nurse education. This requirement is unique in that the previous statutory bodies did not have a statutory obligation, even though they did have a professional and moral obligation. Because of this fundamental duty it is inevitable that the basic pattern of professional education which eventually leads to the provision of qualified nurses, midwives and health visitors must be a changing one. As health care needs of the nation become even more of a challenge to health authorities and their staff, the resources available will need to be used with an ever-increasing efficiency and effectiveness.

There can be no doubt that the structure and content of nursing education will undergo change but the national provision of basic nursing training will continue for as long as the public requires its sick to be cared for. What tends to create a little anxiety is not the provision for basic qualification but the facility for continuing development education from qualification to retirement. If basic nurse education is considered to be expensive the cost of providing continuing education on a regular basis for every qualified nurse employed within a health authority will then, in comparison, seem unaffordable. The profession will have to consider ways of providing up-date, refresher and top-up knowledge and skills at the least possible cost. Perhaps a complete and radical change of attitudes may be necessary if nursing and nurse education are to thrive in the future. Certainly, the question of paying students the equivalent of a salary whilst they are students will be resolved by the introduction of grants and bursaries. Those staff who wish to develop their professional or managerial skills other than as a direct requirement of the authority may have wholly or partly to fund their personal development costs.

The content of nurse education in the last decade of the twentieth century and into the twenty-first century will be a direct reflection of the health care demands prevalent at the time. Process, however, will be very much centred around research appreciation and application, with courses that have a common foundation programme and where health as a concept is preferred to the illness or disease model. Students will not sit for long periods of time behind desks in schools of nursing being fed a diet of theory prior to attempting to make that theory operational in a strange and threatening environment.

There has always been the temptation, not only by nurse educationists but also by nursing service managers, to hold up education as the panacea for all problems and shortcomings. Education can help in both identifying problems and designing solutions, but it is not the sole cure. By far the majority of operational problems at ward or departmental level are not due to professional ignorance or incompetence but are a result of incompetent or ineffectual management. That is not so much a criticism of individual managers but more an indictment of the system that prepares and develops both first-level and intermediary managers.

When periodic registration is linked to the demonstration of competency to practise, through the provision of evidence of continuing education or personal professional development, the emphasis on which current in-service and post-basic education is founded reflects more the needs of the organisation than the personal desires of the employee. This is how it should be, but if in the future the guarantee of having qualified staff is ensured by providing an opportunity for personal professional updating and proficiency then the balance of training provision may be altered.

References

Committee on Nursing (1972) *Report of the Committee on Nursing (Briggs Report)* (Cmd 5115). London: H M S O

Department of Health & Social Security (1979) *The Nurses, Midwives and Health Visitors Act*. London: H M S O

Department of Health & Social Security (1980) *Health Service Development, Structure and Management*, HC(80)8. London: D H S S

Department of Health & Social Security (1983a) *National Health Service Management Enquiry*. London: H M S O

Department of Health & Social Security (1983) *The Nurses, Midwives and Health Visitors Rules Approval Order 1983*. London: D H S S

Department of Health & Social Security (1984) *Implementation of the N H S Management Enquiry Report*, HC(84)13. London: H M S O

Douglas L M (1982) *Nursing Management and Leadership in Action*. St Louis, Mo: Mosby

English National Board (1985) *Professional Education/Training Courses; A Consultation Paper*. London: E N B

General Nursing Council for England & Wales (1974) *A Specification of Nursing Competence* (74/8/16). London: G N C

General Nursing Council for England & Wales (1977) *A Statement of Education Policy* (77/19/A). London: G N C

General Nursing Council for England & Wales (1982a) *Training Syllabus, Register of Nurses, Mental Nursing*. London: G N C

General Nursing Council for England & Wales (1982b) *Training Syllabus, Register of Nurses, Mental Handicap Nursing*. London: G N C

Royal College of Nursing Commission on Nursing Education (1985) *The Education of Nurses: A New Dispensation*. London: R C N

United Kingdom Central Council, Working Group 3 (1982) *Consultation Paper – The Development of Nurse Education*. London: U K C C

United Kingdom Central Council (1986) *Project 2000. A New Preparation for Practice*. London: U K C C

Afterword

The final draft of this book was completed at the time when the Secretary of State was deliberating on health authorities' response to the U K C C's Project 2000 (1986) proposals. Indeed, by the time this book is published the fate of the Council's recommendations will be known. Although no attempt will be made at prediction, it is worth recording that at this time, although many health authorities acknowledge the requirement for fundamental change in nursing and nurse education, few believe that the Council's recommendations are affordable or achievable. Of this scenario Clay (1987) asserts:

> 'A succession of reports over the past 50 years have either been misunderstood, ignored or only partially implemented. Crystal clear, far-sighted recommendations such as those in the Wood Report (1947) were watered down, not primarily by the government but by the profession itself – or sections of it – anxious to preserve the system, nervous of radical change and determined to move only as far as they were pushed.'

An attempt will be made here to survey and discuss those issues that have significant and immediate implications for nursing and, in particular, nurse education, which, it is to be hoped, will serve to orientate and give the reader a sense of future direction. With or without Project 2000, there are major issues that must be addressed and resolved by the profession. Of these, none is more contentious than that relating to the enrolled nurse. The U K C C, the National Boards and the Royal College of Nursing are agreed that, in the future, there should be preparation for one single grade of nurse. It is worth noting that without a change of ruling there has been a dramatic reduction in the number of training places for pupil nurses. In 1982, 11440 pupils entered training; this has been reduced by more than half in the succeeding five years (E N B 1986). This trend may support the authors' assertion that it is no longer justifiable, if it ever was, to recruit so-called 'academically less able' learners, paradoxically provide them with a shorter training and require them to do precisely the same job on qualifying as their registered colleagues for lower remuneration and with strictly limited opportunities for role enhancement and promotion. Those opposed to the abolition of the grade argue, quite correctly, that, particularly at a time of recruitment crisis, the profession cannot afford to preclude those individuals who do not meet the Council's academic entry requirements. However, the broadening of the 'entry gate', particularly for mature entrants, the increased availability of 'access schemes' and greater collaboration between schools of nursing and colleges of further education in preparing young people to enter nursing, combined with an unprejudiced scrutiny of the potential of Youth Training Schemes available to nurse training, may well substantially resolve this problem.

The Nurses' Midwives and Health Visitors Rules Approval Order (1983), Rules 18(1) and 18(2), clarified the competencies of the two grades (D H S S 1983). One significant consequence of this clarification of roles is that it effectively limited the contribution that enrolled nurses could make to the training of students preparing to be Level 1 practitioners. On the issue of student supervision, the Board's education officers quite legitimately questioned: 'Is it possible for a Level 2 nurse to act as a role model for a student for Level 1 practice?'

Approximately one-third of all trained nurses are enrolled. In terms of direct care provision this grade, particularly in the care of the elderly and continuing care environments, are, typically, responsible for 60 per cent or more of care delivered. It is inconceivable that despite the appropriateness of one grade of nurse, the skills and potential of enrolled nurses should be ignored. Whilst those who are unwilling or unable to convert to Level 1 will most certainly have their status protected, the greater challenge is defying convention and education ritual by devising imaginative and innovatory schemes of conversion that are not constrained by bureaucracy and the rigid interpretation of training rules.

The debate concerning the enrolled nurse is a component of a much broader issue — that concerning 'skills mix'. The N H S has always relied upon support staff to work alongside professionally qualified nurses. Demographic trends, the U K C C Project 2000 proposals and increasing scientific scrutiny of nursing skills mix places the role and preparation of the support worker high on health districts's agendas. It is envisaged that the preparation of the support worker should be the responsibility of ' . . . the service, not that of the statutory body' (D H S S 1987). The Department's report recommends that training programmes should be service-led, responding to service needs and involving participation of those in service at the local level. Nurse education and, in particular, individual schools of nursing should not merely assume the role of interested advisers, but should summon their considerable resources and abilities in promoting and developing local training schemes. The D H S S also recommend that: 'There should be a commitment to provide "links and ladders" in the overall training scheme and to ensure that there are no unnecessary barriers to transfer and progression.' There are those individuals well placed in the statutory authorities who are disdainful of the notion that nurse education should be directly involved in the preparation of support workers or in Youth Training Schemes; for them Virginia Henderson's view is salutory: 'There are no menial tasks in nursing — only menial attitudes towards them.'

It is significant that whilst nurse education views association with the Manpower Services Commission, National Health Service Training Authority and technical colleges with guarded suspicion, there is an unguarded enthusiasm for migration into higher education. It would seem that this has more to do with nurse education's self-effacement and poor self-esteem than with concern for the provision of a continuum of vocational training and professional education consistent with society's health care requirements. It is self-evident that nurse education has much to gain by collaborating with universities and polytechnics, not least the academic accreditation of nursing courses that would give nurse 'graduates' access to important opportunities, currently denied by higher education.

> 'We must not assume that the grass is greener on the University campus. Given our nation's economic decline, are we to assume that commerce and industry are uncritical of the science, engineering and management graduates being produced by Higher Education . . . assimilation of Nurse Education into Higher Education would be merely denial of the problem' (Kenworthy & Nicklin 1985).

More crudely — if the measure of success of the location of vocational education was based on the public's esteem and satisfaction, would the universities that prepare our social workers and teachers be more highly regarded than the schools that train our nurses? Resolution and progress may well reside with broader diversification and greater collaboration. The Chairman of the N H S Management Board (Peach 1987) reports:

> 'One of the passages in the original Project 2000 discussion papers excited little debate but has interested me. This was the suggestion that the Common Foundation Programme might form the basis for a common foundation for shared learning with other health workers . . . were we to pursue the idea of shared training further, there could be pay-offs in terms of greater productivity as well as undoubted benefits of a greater shared understanding of the common task.'

The National Health Service is the largest employer of labour in Europe. Half of its employees are in nursing grades. Health care provision and training is massive in scale and cost — possibly this should form a basis of a rationale for the formation of colleges of health. Rather than health care training being randomly located throughout the health service in higher and further education, it should be unified in one institution — in such an enterprise nurse education would have a fundamental and central role.

Any discussion on the future of nurse education that disregards general management would be not only incomplete but inept. The introduction of general management is, as was intended, the most radical change in the Health Service since its inception. With previous reorganisations there has been a tendency for nurse education and schools of nursing to sit on the sidelines, await the new structure and then find somewhere that is a reasonable fit to locate themselves. 'Griffiths' (D H S S 1984) has provided nurse education with an opportunity not only to manage itself effectively but also to contribute effectively to the management of the service. Education managers who do not legitimately exploit this situation not only fail nurse education but also fail the Service and its clients. Management expectations of nurse education have never been higher; to achieve service manpower objectives, Directors of Nurse Education must demand and command unimpeded control of the resources required to accomplish their task. It is entirely consistent with general management philosophy that schools of nursing be perceived as independent units of management and incur the associated privileges and penalties. Indeed, the 'failure' of schools of nursing in the past has been frequently associated with that imcompatible formula of responsibility without authority. Such a situation has also provided convenient refuge for those in nurse education who seek excuses for lack of progress or failure. Such ambiguity of management function has no place in a climate of general management.

Many articles and texts over the past twenty years have claimed that nursing is at 'the crossroads', on 'the threshold', at 'the dawn of a new era' or at a similarly exciting but uncertain location in its evolution. However, it is difficult to conceive of a time when the ability of nurse education to respond to its challenges was so crucial. The *Review of Nursing Skill Mix* (D H S S 1986) reports: 'Our overwhelming impression is that the quality and cost-effectiveness of care depended crucially on the leader of the nursing team.' This is equally true of nurse education; the curricular designers' intentions are only as good as the ability and commitment of 'ward sisters' and their teams to teach and assess students in the clinical setting. At a time of considerable uncertainty, it is absolutely certain that clinical nurses are crucial to the future of nurse education — it is for them this book was written and to whom it is dedicated.

References

Clay T et al (1987) *Nurses, Power and Politics*. London: Heinemann

Department of Health & Social Security (1983) *The Nurses, Midwives and Health Visitors Rules Approval Order 1983*. London: D H S S

Department of Health & Social Security (1984) *Implementation of the N H S Management Enquiry Report*, HC(84)13. London: H M S O

Department of Health & Social Security (1986) *'Mix and Match' — A Review of Nursing Skill Mix*. London: D H S S

Department of Health & Social Security (1987) *Role and Preparation of Support Workers*. London: D H S S

English National Board (1986) *Annual Report 1985/86*. London: E N B

Kenworthy N & Nicklin P J (1985) Is the grass greener on the university campus? *Nursing Mirror*, **160**(18)

Peach L (1987) *Address to R C N Manpower Conference*, May 1987

Index